STAFF DEVELOPMENT:

PRACTICES THAT PROMOTE LEADERSHIP IN LEARNING COMMUNITIES

Sally J. Zepeda
University of Georgia

EYE ON EDUCATION
6 DEPOT WAY WEST, SUITE 106
LARCHMONT, NY 10538
(914) 833–0551
(914) 833–0761 fax

Library of Congress Cataloging-in-Publication Data

Zepeda, Sally., 1956–
    Staff development: practices that promote leadership in learning communities / by Sally J. Zepeda.
        p.   cm. — (The school leadership library)
    Includes bibliographical references and indexes.
    ISBN 1-883001-69-2
        1. Teachers—In-service training—United States. 2. Career development —United States. 3. School personnel management—United States. 4. Educational leadership—United States. I. Title. II. Series.
LB1731.Z47   1999
370'.71'55—dc21   98–48405
                                                                          CIP

10 9 8 7 6 5 4 3 2

Editorial and production services provided by Richard H. Adin Freelance Editorial Services, 9 Orchard Drive, Gardiner, NY 12525 (914-883-5884)

Also Available from EYE ON EDUCATION

**Working in a Legal and Regulatory Environment:
A Handbook for School Leaders**
by David Sperry

**Human Resources Administration:
A School-based Perspective**
by Richard E. Smith

**Money and Schools:
A Handbook for Practitioners**
by David C. Thompson and R. Craig Wood

The Principal as Steward
by Jack McCall

The Principal's Edge
by Jack McCall

**The Reflective Supervisor:
A Practical Guide for Educators**
by Ray Calabrese and Sally Zepeda

Thinking Through the Principalship
by Dianne Ashby and Sam Krug

Hands-on Leadership Tools for Principals
by Ray Calabrese, Gary Short, and Sally Zepeda

**The Administrator's Guide to School–
Community Relations**
by George E. Pawlas

**Data Analysis for Comprehensive
Schoolwide Improvement**
by Victoria L. Bernhardt

**The School Portfolio:
A Comprehensive Framework for School
Improvement**
by Victoria L. Bernhardt

Research on Educational Innovations (2d ed.)
by Arthur K. Ellis and Jeffrey T. Fouts

The School Leadership Library

David A. Erlandson and Alfred P.
Wilson, General Editors

The School Leadership Library, a series of 21 books, shows you what successful principals and other school leaders must know and be able to do. Grounded in best knowledge and practice, these books demonstrate best practices of effective principals. They provide recommendations which can be applied to a school leader's daily work.

Each volume includes practical materials, such as:

- checklists
- sample letters and memos
- model forms
- action plans

What should an effective principal know and be able to do? Members of the National Policy Board for Educational Administration (sponsored by NAESP, NASSP, AASA, ASCD, NCPEA, UCEA, and other professional organizations) developed a set of 21 "domains," or building blocks, that represent the essential knowledge and skills of successful principals. Each volume in this series is dedicated to explaining and applying one of these building blocks.

Contact Eye On Education for more details.

The School Leadership Library

The Functional Domains

Leadership Gary M. Crow, L. Joseph Matthews, and Lloyd E. Mccleary

Information Collection Short, Short, and Brinson, Jnr.

Problem Analysis C.M. Achilles, John Reynolds, and Susan Hoover

Judgment James Sweeney and Diana Bourisaw

Organizational Oversight Erlandson, Stark, and Ward

Implementation Anita M. Pankake

Delegation Michael Ward and Bettye MacPhail

The Programmatic Domains

Instruction and the Learning Environment James Keefe and John Jenkins

Staff Development Sally J. Zepeda

Student Guidance and Development Ward and Worsham

Measurement and Evaluation James F. McNamara and David A. Erlandson

Resource Allocation M. Scott Norton and Larry Kelly

The Interpersonal Domains

Motivating Others David P. Thompson

Interpersonal Sensitivity John R. Hoyle and Harrison M. Crenshaw

Oral and Nonverbal Expression Ivan Muse

Written Expression India J. Podsen, Charles Allen, Glenn Pethel, and John Waide

The Contextual Domains

Working in a Legal and Regulatory Environment: A Handbook for School Leaders David Sperry

* Other titles to follow

ACKNOWLEDGMENTS

There are people who assisted me with this book. R. Stewart Mayers, a doctoral student at the University of Georgia, provided countless hours in the library and assisted me in staying focused. His contributions throughout are gratefully acknowledged. Gayle Harlin-Fischer, Ph.D., assisted with developing the format of the field-based case studies.

I am indebted to the teachers, staff development consultants, principals, and higher education faculty who allowed their practices to be included in this book. These practices are exemplary. Hopefully, their collective voices will be heard by those who want to continue to expand professional development in schools.

Especially inspiring was the phone conversation with Carlene Murphy, a professional staff development consultant in Augusta, Georgia. Her devotion to developing long-term relationships with schools is humbling.

To the reviewers, Gary W. Elmen, Joellen Killion, and Lois A. Stanciak, I am appreciative of your long hours spent reading this manuscript. Your insights were invaluable.

Finally, my appreciation is extended to Dr. David Erlandson, coeditor of the Eye on Education Leadership Series, for his critical and reflective review of the original manuscript.

Sally J. Zepeda
The University of Georgia

ABOUT THE AUTHOR

Dr. Sally J. Zepeda, a former K-12 administrator and teacher, has served as a high school teacher, director of special programs, assistant principal, and principal at the elementary, middle, and high school levels. She is an assistant professor of educational leadership at the University of Georgia. Prior to her appointment to the University of Georgia faculty, she was assistant professor of educational leadership and policy studies at the University of Oklahoma where she also served as Program Area Coordinator of the Educational Administration, Curriculum, and Supervision Program Area. She teaches instructional supervision, teacher evaluation models, supervision of special programs and personnel, and technology for administrators.

Dr. Zepeda has written numerous articles for such journals as the *Journal of Curriculum and Supervision*, the *Journal of Staff Development*, the *Journal of School Leadership*, the *High School Journal*, *NASSP*, the *Oklahoma Journal of Curriculum and Supervision*, *School Business Affairs*, *Wingspan*, and the *Kappa Delta Pi Record*.

She has also coauthored three books: *The Reflective Supervisor: A Practical Guide for Educators* (with Ray Calabrese), *Hands-On Leadership Tools for Principals* (with Ray Calabrese and Gary Short), and *Special Programs in Regular Schools: Historical Foundations, National Standards, and Contemporary Issues* (with Michael Langenbach).

Dr. Zepeda is the book and audio review column editor for the *Journal of Staff Development* and is the editor of the American Educational Research Association's Supervision SIG newsletter. She is a member of the Council of Professors of Instructional Supervision (COPIS), and a life-time Fellow in the Foundation for Excellence in Teaching.

TABLE OF CONTENTS

FOREWORD

For more than two decades staff development and professional growth have been central in our efforts to improve educational practice. While given a central position in school improvement, the quality of in-service learning programs has tended to be mediocre at best. In-service learning programs have generally failed to employ best practices and to apply the research in the field of staff development. As a result, in-service education has had limited effect on classroom practice and student achievement.

In this same 20-year period, we have learned a great deal about staff development from best practices in schools that have successfully improved through the systematic use of effective in-service learning programs. At the same time, more and more research in staff development has been conducted and has added to our understanding of what should be included in an effective program. This book is an excellent effort to present what educators have learned about staff development when the goal is improving school practice and student learning.

Sally Zepeda has examined the major issues in the field of staff development. The first issue she addresses is the key role that the principal plays in instructional improvement and staff development. Clearly, the role of the principal is crucial in ensuring quality staff development and in creating a culture where professional growth and staff development are supported and valued.

Next, she considers the nature of the adult learner and of adult learning. Recognition of the importance of the adult learner and of how he or she learns is important in planning and implementing in-service learning programs that result in both an understanding of the content and of real change in professional practice. Those involved in the design and implementation of staff development programs must understand how adults learn and develop. It is just as important for them as it is for elementary and secondary teachers to understand how their students learn.

The next two topics, organizational learning and job-embedded learning, are relatively new to the field of staff development, yet they may change the way we think about professional learning programs in the next decade. They move the forms of staff development away from structured in-service workshops and toward learning from one's experiences on the job and then sharing those experiences with others in the school. Here, Zepeda presents what we mean by organizational learning and discusses what is essential to creating such learning experiences.

In addition to examining the different components of effective staff development, Zepeda presents the major models that explain the theoretical basis for different kinds of professional growth programs. The five models include those that seem to hold the greatest promise for guiding our thinking about and our planning for staff development. The RPTIM Model, for example, is focused on school-based improvement through staff development. The Individually Guided Model provides a framework for in-service learning designed for individual learners. The Study Groups and Action Research Models clarify the nature of two popular approaches to job-embedded learning. Finally, the Problem-Based Model explains different approaches to using staff development to solve school and instructional problems. Chapter 6 gives the conceptual base for designing and delivering staff development.

One of the major weaknesses in past in-service learning programs has been the superficial nature of the evaluation used to assess the impact of workshops and other professional learning experiences. Zepeda does a nice job of expanding the current view on evaluating staff development. She shows the "what," the "why," and the "how" that are required to assess the effects of in-service learning efforts. She looks at the impact on the participants of staff development and at the effects of such training on student learning.

Zepeda concludes with a discussion of two closely related topics essential for successful staff development: providing adequate funding and allocating human and physical resources.

Having conducted research in the field of staff development for over 25 years, I have read many works on the topic of professional development. I recommend this book without reservation. This is a source that will be turned to frequently as you plan and conduct in-service learning programs that really do make a difference.

Fred H. Wood
Professor of Education,
University of Oklahoma

INTRODUCTION

Staff Development: Practices that Promote Leadership in Learning Communities comes at an exciting time—we are entering a new millennium where growth goes beyond mere staff development. We are hearing a more informed and authoritative voice from teachers and administrators on what is needed to further develop the talents and strengths of the teaching force. This book was first conceptualized as a way to cover the National Standard, Staff Development, in the Eye on Education Leadership Series. Shortly after my initial conversation with the series coeditor, Professor David Erlandson, I was struck by the very personal and professional nature of staff development. I reflected long and deep on effective staff development practices that I have seen both teachers and administrators design, and on the long-term positive effects of their collective efforts. This insight drew me back to the field, visiting schools in a different way—not as a former teacher or administrator, or now a university researcher, but rather as a learner. Principals and teachers confirmed my conviction—people want to belong to a school that is a learning community. Such schools are hubs of learning; they are the beacons of light. The community members are commanders of change.

The two unifying themes in this book are change and the vital role of the principal in setting in motion the conditions that will enhance and extend learning for adults. I have tried to balance research, practical applications, and theory. Hopefully, these three areas will assist practicing principals, those aspiring to the principalship, staff development directors, department chairs, and teachers alike, because they are all leaders in a learning community.

Sally J. Zepeda
The University of Georgia

PREFACE

The school, as a human organization, cannot exceed the boundaries created by the synergistic behavior of the people in it, and the principal has a key role in working with teachers to expand these boundaries to their fullest limits. In this book, Sally Zepeda develops this role in the context of the school as a learning community, in which every member is a learner and is committed to his or her own learning as well as to the learning of other members of the community. In the learning community, the principal shares leadership with teachers and other professionals as they seek to maximize the learning capacity of the school. If their effort is to be successful, staff development must not simply be "delivered" but must be adapted to the learning needs and opportunities of the learners to whom it is directed. *Staff Development: Practices that Promote Leadership in Learning Communities* effectively describes strategies for accomplishing this.

The text is divided into eight chapters. Each chapter examines a staff development area or process: professional standards, the role of the principal, adult learners, learning communities, job-embedded learning, staff development models, evaluating staff development, and funding.

Within each chapter, the knowledge base of each area is presented along with the processes embedded within it. Also, most chapters have *Notes From the Field* where the work of principals who are instructional leaders is highlighted. The knowledge base and practices are balanced to help the reader to begin thinking of the possibilities within a specified context. Each chapter, except Chapter 1, has a detailed *Case Study From the Field* that gives the reader an expanded description of a program that has yielded positive results. The schools that are profiled include the name of the principal, the school, and contact information. The hope is to keep the discussion of best practices continuing during and after you finish the book. Each chapter also has accompanying *Questions* to help you consider even further the applicability to your own site. Finally, each chapter has a *Suggested Readings* section.

Chapter 1 discusses the standards that emanate from such organizations as the National Staff Development Council (NSDC) and the National Council for Accreditation of Teacher Education (NCATE). These standards serve as a base for designing staff development initiatives because they lay the foundation for the types of process, application, and context information to be considered in emerging designs.

Chapter 2 focuses on the role of the principal as an instructional leader in providing opportunities for staff development. Leadership is explored in relation to the principal's responsibility for framing the right mindset for professional development. You are led through a discussion about recognizing the markers of a school's culture and about uncovering organizational learning barriers that can possibly stymie efforts.

Chapter 3 focuses on the unique needs of adult learners and on how the principal can set the conditions that provide more appropriate staff development opportunities for teachers.

Chapter 4 focuses on building learning communities for adults. The attributes of learning communities are explored in relation to emerging research and practices from the field.

Chapter 5 explores job-embedded learning and its essential ingredients: relevance, transfer of practice, time, and feedback. This chapter charts a more expansive view of staff development—growth and learning are joined in a more systematic way to the daily work of teachers.

Chapter 6 describes the most commonly utilized staff development models and the processes inherent in them. No particular model is emphasized over the other. In fact, you are encouraged to be eclectic in using these models as a springboard to develop more context-specific models of staff development.

Chapter 7 focuses on evaluating the results of staff development to assess these efforts and to assist in modifying and planning future staff development activities that will unify prior and future initiatives.

Chapter 8 deals with the thorny issues surrounding funding and resource allocation. Alternative strategies for staff development—grant writing, working with foundations, business partnerships, and the role of the principal as entrepreneur—are explored.

Staff Development: Practices that Promote Leadership in Learning Communities is a welcome addition to the School Leadership Library and to the general literature on school leadership. Too often "staff development" has been seen as something that is added on at the end of the day or at certain predesignated times of the year in order to fit our scheduling needs rather than the needs of the learners. This important book refocuses our goals for staff development and provides the tools for attaining those goals.

David A. Erlandson
Alfred P. Wilson

1

TOWARD DEFINING STAFF DEVELOPMENT: UNDERSTANDING THE STANDARDS

Learning is but an adjunct to ourself.
William Shakespeare,
Two Gentlemen of Verona

Staff development, in-service education, and training are terms that are often used interchangeably in educational arenas. Are these words synonymous with one another? That depends! This ambiguity is not very comforting whether you are in a principal preparation program, a newly hired principal or assistant principal, a middle school team leader, a high school department chair, or a district level administrator. Staff development is the chameleon of public education; it can adapt itself in shape or size to fit the need it is asked to address. It is a process and a content that hangs onto a knowledge base. Staff development is a process which principals and teachers need to master.

Corporations have recognized for years the need to maintain in-house training programs. New technologies, products, and services require that the corporation's human resources be informed concerning their use and implementation. There are obvious parallels between professional development in business and staff development within public education. Both are based on research concerning

1

adult learning, both are designed to meet specific needs, and both are financed from within. Education, however, has standards in place. That is the thrust of this chapter.

CHAPTER OBJECTIVES

♦ Compare and contrast staff development, in-service, and training.
♦ Present the staff development standards.

COMPARISON OF STAFF DEVELOPMENT, IN-SERVICE, AND TRAINING

WHY DO WE DEFINE STAFF DEVELOPMENT?

First, public schools across the United States spend more money on personnel than on anything else. This investment needs to be protected and nurtured. Second, staff development has a direct impact on the quality of instruction. Third, staff development is oriented toward facilitating growth in individuals as well as in the organization. Where growth ceases, atrophy tends to begin (Day, 1981).

DEFINITIONS OF STAFF DEVELOPMENT

Attitudes and perspectives concerning staff development have changed through the years. Dewey (1938) believed the educative process could be understood "in terms of the active participle, *growing*" (p. 36, emphasis in the original). Campbell, Corbally, and Ramseyer (1958) describe in-service training as "professional improvement" (p. 209). Nicholson, Joyce, Parker, and Waterman (1976) analyzed over 2,000 documents concerning teacher in-service for the purpose of extrapolating a comprehensive definition. The one descriptor found to be essential in defining teacher in-service was *continuity*. This finding seriously weakens the validity of the one-shot approach to professional development. Principals can provide leadership in achieving continuity by examining some broad concepts. The principal is encouraged to examine:

- *Orientation of training:* What need will it address?
- *Clientele to be served:* Whose need is to be served?
- *Agency effected:* Who is to be trained?
- *Financing the program:* Who will pay the cost for the training? (Orlich, 1989a, p. 5)

Orlich (1989a, p. 5) believes that:

> In-service education denotes programs or activities that are based on identified needs; that are collaboratively planned and designed for a specific group of individuals in the school district; that have a very specific set of learning objectives and activities; and that are designed to extend, add, or improve immediate job-oriented skills, competencies, or knowledge with the employer paying the cost.

STAFF DEVELOPMENT VS. TRAINING

During the 1980s and 1990s, both the business and the education arena began placing importance on the development of their human resources. Employee training began taking the form of isolated events. Epperly and Cohen (1984) describe training as "interventions…to enhance skills" (p. 88). Laird (1985) offers that training is "…an experience which causes people to acquire new, predetermined behaviors" (p. 11).

In contrast, staff development has been described in terms of an ongoing, systematic process. Fullan (1982) indicates that staff development is "…ongoing, interactive, cumulative learning necessary to develop new conceptions, skills, and behaviors" (p. 66). Bradley, Kallik, and Regan (1991) offer that staff development is a "…systematic attempt to affect the professional practices, beliefs and understandings of school persons toward an announced goal" (p. 3).

STAFF DEVELOPMENT VS. IN-SERVICE

Staff development is not intended to be a remedial or deficit model that fixes errors. It is much more complex. Staff development is concerned with building the climate for growth and success. Staff development is a lifelong pursuit to improve the quality of education (Chell, 1995).

There are several innate differences between in-service and staff development. Orlich (1989a) believes that in-service is more job oriented; staff development is more person and process oriented. In-service has immediacy and is implemented to improve job-related skills. Conversely, staff development, albeit job-embedded (Wood & Killian, 1998), provides thoughtful and guided enhancement of human talents and focuses on the attainment of long-range goals. Finally, although in-service focuses on a specific group of individuals (i.e., subject matter, special education teachers), staff development targets the entire staff, adopting the philosophy that the school is a "community of learners" (Blase & Blase, 1998). Hass (1957) states that "...staff development promotes the continuous improvement of the total professional staff of the school system" (p. 13).

WHY STAFF DEVELOPMENT IS NEEDED

Danielson (1996) indicates that "continuing development is the mark of a true professional, an ongoing effort that is never completed. Educators committed to attaining and remaining at the top of their profession invest much energy in staying informed and increasing their skills" (p. 115). For the principal, providing staff development is:

+ A moral responsibility to set the conditions for adults to grow; and,

+ Essential because the organization will grow to its fullest capacity when teachers are empowered to make changes.

Teachers need to have a tremendous voice—they need to be heard and supported in their learning endeavors. Staff development must be grounded in a carefully conceived and clearly stated sense of purpose and be embedded in core beliefs that are under constant scrutiny by the members of the learning community. These core beliefs and sense of purpose will allow teachers to listen to their voices guide them in creating learning opportunities for themselves, their students, and the organization. In *The Courage to Teach* (1998), Palmer writes: "The only way to get out of trouble is to go in deeper. We must enter, not evade, the tangles of teaching so we can understand them better and negotiate them with more grace …to serve our children well" (p. 2).

The principal's role is to assist teachers in finding their "learning" voices. Without continuous growth for adults, students are shortchanged: "What teachers know and can do is the most important influence on what students learn" (*Report of the National Commission on Teaching and America's Future* 1996, p. iv). The Report concludes: "…schools that have found ways to educate all students well have done so by providing ongoing learning for teachers and staff " (p. 9). Teachers are their own "raw materials" (Bennis, 1989, p. 40). An awareness of self promotes growth through internal reflection and self-analysis. Couple this type of self-discovery with dialogue among peers and the principal will see a strong community of learners emerge.

THE "CONSTANT" VARIABLES OF STAFF DEVELOPMENT

Caldwell (1989) presents the nested nature of staff development as having three "constant" variables: context, content, and process. A staff development initiative should be planned for the purpose of addressing a set of specifically identified needs. These needs provide the "context" for that initiative. Within this context, the "contents" for the initiative are selected. The "processes" are the sequence of events that occur within the structure of the chosen staff development model.

THE CONTEXT

The context of staff development has changed radically over the past decade. Historically, the school improvement process began with the board of education selecting a number of goals depicting the major educational aspirations or problems within a district. The central office staff would then prioritize these goals and select programs for staff development that most closely related to the identified needs. From this, principals would lead their staff through a systematic program selection process and develop a site plan for staff development based on the broad goals set by the district. Often, staff development experts were called in to assist principals as they planned and implemented programs to achieve specific improvements. Professional staff developers, while valuable in providing technical assistance, were distantly removed from the school site. Caldwell (1989) envisioned the cutting edge of staff development to be "...the facilitation of improvement goals and programs developed by the faculty of individual schools" (p. 52).

Building an atmosphere of shared decision-making and collective responsibility among principals and teachers enhances professional development initiatives (Blase & Blase, 1998). The context of staff development has, therefore, changed from focusing on problems and goals at the district level to contextualizing staff development programs according to the specific needs of schools. Principals have become key individuals in implementing effective staff development programs (Bell, 1986; Chell, 1995; Rutherford, 1989).

THE CONTENT

Content, as applied to staff development, can be defined in two ways. The first application concerns the substance of what is contained. The models and processes utilized to effect change are discussed later in Chapter 6. Content may also be defined as the extent, size, or capacity of the container we call staff development. Principals need to understand the intended vastness of staff development as opposed to the confined notion of in-service training.

THE PROCESS

Process is defined as a series of actions, which lead to the accomplishment of some result. Staff development is a succession of strategies planned and implemented for the purpose of effecting change. The nature of the desired change can be the improvement of existing practice, the implementation of new practice, the introduction of new curriculum objectives, or the induction of new faculty members. In 1989, Rutherford interpreted staff development as "any effort to improve the professional performance of school staff members...," and Joyce and Showers (1995), cited by Blase and Blase (1998), explained "[that staff development is] a system ensuring that educational professionals regularly enhance their academic knowledge, professional performance, and image as professionals..." (p. 48).

PERSPECTIVES OF STAFF DEVELOPMENT: WHAT DO THE STANDARDS TELL US?

THE NEED FOR STANDARDS

Once our world was much less complicated than today. Families moved less frequently, value systems were generally constant, and the authority of the school and the individuals within the educational system were seldom questioned or criticized. The opportunity to receive an education was considered a privilege, and school curricula were clearly not designed to meet the needs of *all* students. However, in today's diverse and complex world, there is little commonality of objective, much dissatisfaction with public education, and high, but often unrealistic, expectations for meeting the needs of everyone in the educational system (Dillon-Peterson, 1981). For these reasons, it became necessary to develop standards that addressed the continuous professional growth of educators.

NATIONAL STAFF DEVELOPMENT COUNCIL STANDARDS

In 1997, the National Staff Development Council (NSDC) released standards that include context, process, and content competencies for the elementary, middle, and high school levels. For illustrative purposes, an abbreviated form of the NSDC standards is presented here with permission of the National Staff Development Council, Oxford, Ohio. You are encouraged to access the full standards by visiting the National Staff Development Council's Web site: www.nsdc.org.

- ♦ Context

  Effective staff development...

  - Requires and fosters the norm of continuous improvement;

- Requires strong leadership in order to obtain continuing support and to motivate all staff, school board members, parents, and the community to be advocates for continuous improvement;
- Is aligned with the school's and the district's strategic plan and is funded by a line item in the budget;
- Provides adequate time during the work day for staff members to learn and work together to accomplish the school's mission and goals; and,
- Is an innovation in itself that requires study of the change process.

♦ Process

Effective staff development...

- Provides knowledge, skills, and attitudes regarding organization development and systems thinking;
- Is based on knowledge about human learning and development;
- Provides for the three phases of the change process: initiation, implementation, and institutionalization;
- Bases priorities on a careful analysis of disaggregated student data regarding goals for student learning;
- Uses content that has proven value in increasing student learning and development;
- Provides a framework for integrating innovations and relating those innovations to the mission of the organization;
- Requires an evaluation process that is ongoing, includes multiple sources of information, and focuses on all levels of the organization;

- Uses a variety of staff development approaches to accomplish the goals of improving instruction and student success;
- Provides the follow up necessary to ensure improvement;
- Requires staff members to learn and apply collaborative skills to conduct meetings, make shared decisions, solve problems, and work collegially; and,
- Requires knowledge and use of the stages of group development to build effective, productive, collegial teams.

◆ Content

Effective staff development…

- Increases administrators' and teachers' understanding of how to provide school environments and instruction that are responsive to the developmental needs of students;
- Facilitates the development and implementation of school and classroom-based management which maximizes student learning;
- Addresses diversity by providing awareness and training related to the knowledge, skills, and behaviors needed to ensure that an equitable and quality education is provided to all students;
- Enables educators to provide challenging, developmentally appropriate interdisciplinary curricula that engage students in integrative ways of thinking and learning;
- Prepares teachers to use research-based teaching strategies appropriate to their instructional objectives and their students;
- Prepares educators to demonstrate high expectations for student learning;

- Facilitates staff collaboration with and support of families for improving student performance;
- Prepares teachers to use various types of performance assessment in their classrooms;
- Prepares educators to combine academic student learning goals with service to the community;
- Increases administrators' and teachers' ability to provide guidance and advisement to students; and,
- Increases staff knowledge and practice of interdisciplinary team organization and instruction.

(*Author's Note:* The last three content standards are written primarily for secondary schools.)

COMMONALITIES AMONG THE NATIONAL STAFF DEVELOPMENT COUNCIL STANDARDS

Although the National Staff Development Council (NSDC) standards are divided into three groupings—elementary, middle level, and high school—several common themes are evident. Based on NSDC standards, staff development is:

- *Ongoing:* staff development is never really completed;
- *Collaborative:* the entire school community (i.e., teachers, administrators, support staff, parents, and patrons) needs to be involved;
- *Research based:* strategies and practices chosen for implementation have a foundation in research;
- *Driven by data-based decision-making:* data collected, organized, and analyzed are used as a basis for making decisions; and,

♦ Supported with adequate resources: release time and funding are necessary for quality staff development.

The only differences between the NSDC standards for elementary, middle, and high school levels are the age groups defined for purposes of determining appropriateness of teaching and assessment strategies. Sparks and Hirsh (1997) reflect the commonalities of the NSDC standards in their vision. They have identified paradigm shifts in staff development from:

♦ Individual development to individual development *and* organizational development;

♦ Fragmented, piecemeal improvement efforts to staff development driven by a clear, coherent strategic plan for the school district, each school, and the departments that serve schools;

♦ District-focused to school-focused approaches to staff development;

♦ A focus on adult needs and satisfaction to a focus on student needs and learning outcomes, and changes in on-the-job training;

♦ Training conducted away from the job as the primary delivery system for staff development to multiple forms of job-embedded learning;

♦ An orientation toward the transmission of knowledge and skills to teachers by "experts" to the study by teachers of the teaching and learning processes;

♦ Focus on generic instructional skills to a combination of generic and content-specific skills;

♦ Staff developers who function primarily as trainers to those who provide consultation, planning, and facilitation services as well as training;

♦ Staff development provided by one or two departments to staff development as a critical function and major responsibility performed by all administrators and teacher-leaders;

♦ Staff development directed toward teachers as the primary recipients to continuous improvement in performance for everyone who affects student learning; and,

♦ Staff development as a "frill" that can be cut during difficult financial times to staff development as an indispensable process without which schools cannot hope to prepare young people for citizenship and productive employment. (pp. 12–16)

THE NATIONAL COUNCIL FOR THE ACCREDITATION OF TEACHER EDUCATION

The National Council for the Accreditation of Teacher Education (NCATE) provides standards to guide university preparation of educators. NCATE is governed by the education profession, both practicing and preparation personnel, and by other stakeholders in the outcomes of professional teacher preparation programs. The essential mission of NCATE is to provide professional judgment regarding the quality of teacher preparation programs and to encourage continuous improvement (NCATE, 1997).

Within Area II, *Instructional Leadership*, NCATE standards require, in part, that school leaders:

♦ Develop collaboratively a learning organization that supports instructional improvement, builds an appropriate curriculum, and incorporates best practice;

♦ Work with faculty and the stakeholders to identify needs for professional development, to organize, facilitate, and evaluate professional development programs, to integrate district and school priorities, to build faculty as resource, and to ensure that professional development activities focus on improving student outcomes;

♦ Apply adult learning strategies to professional development;

♦ Formulate and implement a self-development plan, endorsing the value of career-long growth and utilizing a variety of resources for continuing professional development. (pp. 22–24)

The NCATE standards mirror the National Policy Board Standards. These two prominent organizations, along with such organizations as the University Council of Educational Administration (UCEA), the National Staff Development Council (NSDC), the National Association of Secondary School Principals (NASSP), and the National Association of Elementary School Principals (NAESP), support similar staff development standards for growth and learning.

INTERSTATE SCHOOL LEADERS LICENSURE CONSORTIUM

Two important elements of the NSDC and NCATE standards are also addressed in the Interstate School Leaders Licensure Consortium (ISLLC) standards: collaboration and continuous learning by both students and staff. In part, these standards define an effective school administrator as someone who promotes the success of all students by:

♦ Facilitating the development, articulation, implementation, and stewardship of a vision of learning that is shared and supported by the school community; and,

♦ Advocating, nurturing, and sustaining a school culture and instructional program conducive to student learning and staff professional growth. (ISLLC, 1997, p. 24)

From these standards, the workings of effective staff development need to be tailored to fit the unique and emerging needs of schools. The principal is encouraged to engage all members of the community in setting in motion the standards presented in this chapter.

WHERE DO WE GO FROM HERE?

For principals on the threshold of the twenty-first century, the mandate is clear: schools that succeed are schools in which every participant is a learner. Atrophy and stagnation begin where growth ceases. The principal is the *point of convergence* for all that the school is and does. He or she sets the tenor of all facets of the school curriculum. Students, teachers, and staff reflect the direction and motivation demonstrated by the principal. The most effective way a principal can motivate faculty members to be active learners is to be active in his or her own learning.

SUMMARY

In this chapter, standards from a variety of sources have been examined. However, a consistent picture emerges. Staff development is:

+ An ongoing process, not a once-a-year event;
+ Everyone involved as leaders and followers;
+ Driven by data-based decision-making;
+ Research based; and,
+ A worthy investment of resources.

In this book, many roles of the principal are discussed: instructional leader, facilitator of learning, manager of resources, mediator, supervisor, and evaluator. The specific responsibilities within these roles as they apply to the administration of a site level staff development program are presented in greater detail in the ensuing chapters.

QUESTIONS

APPLICATION OF STAFF DEVELOPMENT PRINCIPLES

+ The National Staff Development Council (NSDC) provides a framework for viewing staff development: Context, Process, and Content. Examine the staff development activities in the building in which you work and make a list that identifies each activity relative to Content, Process, and Context. Are there any patterns to the types of content, process, and context? What do these patterns indicate?

♦ Examine the standards of NCATE and NSCD. If your state has staff development standards, how do they compare to those of NCATE and NSCD?

ACTION RESEARCH

♦ Visit with the district-level person responsible for directing and coordinating staff development. What is the district's direction? What is the school site's direction? Can both directions complement one another? Should they?

PUTTING STAFF DEVELOPMENT INTO A CONTEXT

♦ Based on the staff development activities in the building in which you work, are these activities in-service, training, or staff development? Be prepared to show examples that support your response.

SUGGESTED READINGS

Caldwell, S. (1989). Introduction. In Caldwell, S. (Ed.), *Staff development: A handbook of effective practices* (pp. 9–13). Oxford, OH: National Staff Development Council.

Orlich, D. (1989). *Staff development*. Needham Heights, MA: Allyn & Bacon.

Sparks, D., & Hirsh S. (1997). *A new vision for staff development*. Alexandria, VA: Association for Supervision and Curriculum Development and Oxford, OH: National Staff Development Council.

2

THE ROLE OF THE PRINCIPAL IN PROVIDING STAFF DEVELOPMENT

Leadership and learning are indispensable to one another.

John F. Kennedy

Chapter 1 led you through the myriad definitions of staff development and the differences between in-service and training. The professional standards that undergird best practices, along with the technical aspects of staff development, were also presented. The content of every chapter hinges on the principal as the instructional leader.

The role of the principal as instructional leader is under much debate as research on this topic has doubled over the past few years. As schools forge ahead with restructuring efforts, the voices of teachers as professionals are, rightfully, growing stronger. The principal is hard pressed not to look deep inside himself or herself to reflect upon the impact staff development can have on the professional lives of teachers.

This chapter explores leadership within the context of assisting the principal to frame staff development initiatives. Without leadership from both teachers and administrators, there is little hope that staff development will make a significant impact on individual and organizational growth. Staff development is about growth and change.

CHAPTER OBJECTIVES

- ◆ Review instructional leadership qualities as they relate to staff development.
- ◆ Uncover how culture building enhances staff development.
- ◆ Recognize organizational barriers to staff development.

THE PRINCIPAL AS INSTRUCTIONAL LEADER

Public school effectiveness has been a topic of emphasis since the early 1980s (Murphy, 1990). Characteristics of effective schools as stated by Sweeney (1982) and Edmonds (1982) include the principal's attention to the quality of instruction, a pervasive and broadly understood instructional vision, and high expectations for student achievement. Brennan and Brennan (1988) indicate that the principal is the most visible school administrator to parents and the ultimate authority to faculty and students.

Principals serve as interpreters and implementors of district policy, and, as such, are responsible for the establishment and maintenance of the overall educational operation of the school. However, the primary responsibility of the principal is the improvement of instruction, and the majority of the principal's time should be spent on curriculum and staff development (Murphy, 1990). The term "instructional leader" clearly describes the role of principals in the quest for excellence in schools (Richardson, Flanigan, & Blackbourn, 1991).

CHARACTERISTICS OF INSTRUCTIONAL LEADERS

A meta-analysis of studies that examined successful instructional leaders (Ellis, 1986) identifies several basic practices and priorities that effective leaders share. The findings suggest that effective instructional leaders:

- ◆ Develop programs based not only on their own personal beliefs and values, but also, based upon their knowledge and understanding of the specific needs of their schools and communities;

♦ Set high expectations within their schools and re-inforce them through daily interactions with staff and students;

♦ Promote collaboration; and,

♦ Cultivate mutual trust among their teachers.

Thurston, Clift, and Schacht (1993) identify four attrib-utes of effective instructional leaders. They indicate that ef-fective leaders are child-centered and focus on the needs of all children. Effective leaders replace the top-down style of administration with an attitude of collaboration among all their constituents. They believe that effective leaders em-brace a strong knowledge base in a variety of contexts and can collect, organize, and present information to teachers, parents, and other interested parties. Finally, as Thurston and his associates (1993) explain, "the leader's significance is not defined by positional authority; the leader's influence is pro-portionate to the ability to communicate the meaningfulness and appropriateness of decisions and actions" (p. 263). Effec-tiveness in school leadership is characterized by an orienta-tion toward continuous learning. If learning is a life-long pur-suit and the goal is to constantly improve education, then educators, too, must be continually engaged in updating their knowledge and skills. Instructional leaders ensure that learning is tailored to the school's context and needs (Thur-ston et al., 1993). Every school is comprised of individu-als—students, teachers, support staff, and parents—who re-flect their own characteristics, beliefs, and attitudes. Each school site has its own unique context, climate, and culture. When combined—context, climate, culture, and characteris-tics—the values of the organization can be better understood.

ACCEPTING THE RESPONSIBILITY FOR STAFF DEVELOPMENT

As the instructional leader, responsibility for effective staff development programs rests primarily with the princi-pal (Rutherford, 1989), and "of the many roles the principal must play, the role…of staff development deserves the high-est priority" (McCall, 1997, p. 23). As staff developer, the principal realizes that "the actual process of learning that teachers go through is as important, if not more important, than the teaching they do in the classroom. *Students learn only from teachers who are themselves in the process of learning"* (McCall, 1997, p. 23, emphasis in the original).

FRAMING THE RIGHT MIND-SET

Schlechty (1990), cited in Crow, Matthews, and McCleary (1996), indicates that "the school principal is one leader in a context of leadership—a 'leader of leaders' " (p. 32). From the work in the field, this common reference signals the principal as a "teacher of teachers," providing developmentally appropriate learning opportunities. One might think the concept of the principal as a teacher of teachers a demeaning one but such a perception depends on how the principal approaches the provision of staff development, how the principal supports change and innovation, and how the principal engages and interacts with teachers as they pursue activities that promote growth.

DEVELOPING LEADERSHIP

A cooperative mind-set coupled with certain leadership qualities can promote professional development. In *The Constructivist Leader* (1995), Lambert and her associates explore the nature of leadership from the perspective of the principal moving away from having *"to do things to or for others"* (p. 30, emphasis added). Lambert asserts that constructivist leaders know that "adults in a community can work together to construct meaning and knowledge" (p. 32). They also believe that the constructivist leadership style is "reciprocal…[and as a result]…participants in an educational community [can] …construct meanings…that lead toward a common purpose of schooling" (p. 32).

ESSENTIAL LEADERSHIP QUALITIES

♦ *Reciprocity* is a mutual or cooperative interchange between people. For staff development and other growth oriented activities to work, principals need a leadership style that holds all that comprise the community in equal esteem.

♦ *Followership* Effective principals are secure in their leadership approaches; they can be both a leader and a follower: "This more dynamic sharing feature makes leadership a community endeavor" (Crow, Matthews, & McCleary, 1996, p. 31).

Sergiovanni (1992) believes that "followers are people committed to purposes, a cause, a vision of what the school is and can become, beliefs about teaching and learning, values and standards to which they adhere, and [they have] convictions" (p. 71). Why would a principal want to be both a leader and a follower? The answer is complex; however, Sergiovanni captures the value of being both a leader and follower:

> When followership and leadership are joined, the traditional hierarchy of the school is upset. It changes from a fixed form, with superintendents and principals at the top and teachers and students at the bottom, to one that is in flux. The only constant is that neither superintendents and principals nor teachers and students are at the apex; that position is reserved for the ideas, values, and commitments at the heart of followership. Further, a transformation takes place, and emphasis shifts from bureaucratic, psychological, and technical-rational authority to professional and moral authority. As a result, hierarchical position and personality are not enough to earn one the mantle of leader. Instead, it comes through one's demonstrated devotion and success as a follower. The true leader is the one who follows first. (pp. 71–72)

♦ *Courage* helps effective principals to steer the school in a direction, even if tough decisions need to be made, while removing obstacles that might get in the way of achieving goals.

UNCOVERING AND RECOGNIZING THE MARKERS OF A SCHOOL'S CULTURE

To better understand the school's culture, effective principals look for artifacts, practices, and expectations within the organization. These sources can assist the principal in uncovering and understanding the school's culture. The principal is encouraged to engage faculty, parents, support staff, students, and central administrators who come into frequent contact with the school (e.g., curriculum coordinators and staff development directors) in uncovering the culture of the school. The principal can begin to uncover the school's culture by asking these questions:

- What do people celebrate? How do they celebrate?

- What types of award assemblies does the school plan? Who is involved in the planning and organizing of these events? Who typically attends these events? When are they held (during the school day where the entire community meets or in the evening)?

- Where is student work displayed (in the halls, classrooms, library, main office)?

- Does the school have a mascot? What is the mascot and what does it represent?

- Are student trophies and awards publicly displayed where people can see them?

The principal should seek evidence (e.g., artifacts) to substantiate his or her answers. The principal is encouraged to develop his or her own list, accounting for the individual context of the school site. The value of working with the faculty in identifying the culture of the school is to engage them in dialogue so that a common understanding can emerge. Through discussion and reflection, members of the community develop a common language or lexicon that is embedded with deeper meaning and understanding emanating from the "talk." It is important for the principal to remember that the school is a learning organization and that learning is best achieved when people can work openly with one another, regardless of the task. Given this importance, the principal needs to shift attention to examining the school's culture in terms of adult learning, staff development, and professional growth.

The examination can start by reflecting generally on the learning opportunities that are made available to teachers both formally and informally. After identifying these formal and informal staff development activities, they can be examined in relation to the opportunities they provide for:

♦ Learning

Do teachers, on their own, seek out learning opportunities offered at the site, the district, or externally (graduate school, local and national conferences, workshops)?

♦ Sharing

Do teachers share their knowledge and expertise with other teachers? Do they have a forum for "bringing home" what they have learned in professional development activities?

♦ Reflecting and Discussing

Do teachers openly discuss what they have learned or what they are in the process of discovering about their own teaching practices?

♦ Examining the Talk Over Time

Are discussions held over a sustained period of time? One-shot discussions, like one-shot staff development events, are equally useless in promoting professional growth.

♦ Reading the Word

Are books, professional journals, and technology utilized as resources? Are these resources readily available to teachers and staff (e.g., secretaries and custodians)?

♦ Celebrating

Are teachers honored and recognized for their achievements both in school-related activities and in personal achievements (e.g., finishing a masters degree or receiving recognition from a civic association)?

NOTES FROM THE FIELD

A middle school principal redesigned the faculty lounge to include the professional development library. He enlisted the support of the library media specialist, the lead teacher, and team level leaders to examine what materials were available and what would be needed to promote the interest of the entire staff. After securing the funds and other resources from the district and the parent organization, teachers were polled about what materials would promote their own development. Journals, books, and other print and nonprint materials were ordered. Teachers no longer had to make a special trip to the media center to checkout books; they only had to sign a log in the lounge.

The design of the faculty lounge included new bookshelves, comfortable furniture, and lamps. For Christmas every year, the administrative team buys the faculty a present—a nicely framed painting of school age children. The results of these efforts are clear. Teachers were reading professional materials, discussing common interests, and finding new professional interests. Teachers began bringing reading materials from their own home libraries. The principal began sharing leadership articles from journals he read. After staff development activities, he provided materials to complement and extend relevant topics. To this day, when a teaching candidate interviews for a position, the first stop on the building tour is the faculty lounge, which is now referred to as the professional development lounge by the teachers in this learning community.

UNCOVERING ORGANIZATIONAL LEARNING BARRIERS WITHIN THE SCHOOL SITE

The principal's investigation of the organization's culture can be enhanced by identifying organizational barriers that might impede learning opportunities. The culture of the school is a reflection of the organization; therefore, both opportunities and barriers should be examined together.

Through such an approach, the principal can, perhaps, gain a more thorough understanding of the importance of culture in relation to staff development. Often schools, especially ones with high student enrollment and an equally large teaching staff, become fragmented by sheer size. Regardless of the location of the school (urban, suburban, or rural), teachers and administrators are often flooded with policies and procedures that are essential to the organization. Policies and procedures reflect local, state, and federal "rules and regulations," and union agreements. The principal is bound by mandates, to be sure. However, principals have some latitude in how policies and procedures are enacted within their own buildings.

UNIVERSAL ISSUES THAT IMPACT SCHOOLS

Consider some of the enormous pressures put on schools and their teachers:

♦ Accountability: standardized test scores, rankings within the community, number of graduates attending college and receiving scholarships;

♦ Large class size: most schools out of necessity need to "fill" classes;

♦ Safety issues: violence is making schools unsafe places;

♦ Unique needs of students: more schools are becoming inclusive that is, special needs students are being integrated into regular classrooms;

♦ Technology: with the press for technology, schools are on their way to the information highway;

♦ New developments in the field: teachers are constantly being presented with new developments within the knowledge base of their fields, new approaches to teaching, and new information on how children learn;

♦ Changes in the teaching force: the numbers of alternatively certified teachers and of newly-hired

teachers are increasing due to the greying of the
profession;

♦ Demographics: changes in boundaries, "white
flight," and poverty add pressure and stress to organizations; and,

♦ Restructuring and site-based management: en-
larged roles for teachers and principals can create
workplace challenges that can cause stress.

Organizational barriers often signal excessively bureaucratic and hierarchical leadership patterns that impede staff
development initiatives. Bureaucratic leadership approaches
to solving problems "impose even more fragmented struc-
tures of thought on their members and do not really encourage employees to think for themselves...clearly...fragment-
ing interest in and knowledge about what the organization is
doing" (Morgan, 1986, p. 89).

Regardless of the structure, effective principals see that
teachers and others in the community can connect individual
work with collective goals, objectives, and the school mission. By purposefully sharing information and giving teachers a voice in planning, all members of the school community
can be on the "same page," with united efforts on schoolwide
improvement and professional development.

There are many dilemmas that teachers face, but "...sen-
sitive principals are aware of these workplace dilemmas and
try to alter their schools, from routine, noninspiring places
where the work is drudgery, to joyful centers of learning.
Principals...empower and challenge the intellect and create
an inner glow of professional well-being within each teacher
and staff member..." (Hoyle & Crenshaw, 1997, p. 38).

Organizational barriers are rooted in isolation, ineffective
communication patterns, and in boundaries protected as
turfs.

ISOLATION

Because of the compartmentalized structure of schools,
separation of people by departments and grade levels often
impedes organizational growth. A major byproduct of separation is isolation. Job descriptions provided to teachers am-

plify the expectation that almost every minute of their day is counted—duty periods before, during, and after school. Planning periods are often not coordinated among teachers who could possibly work together if given the opportunity. Lunch breaks are often used for returning parent calls, providing tutoring for individual students, and filling out forms. These conditions create organizational roadblocks.

COMMUNICATION CHANNELS

Establishing open channels of communication enhances the organization. Roberts (1991) indicates that "professional growth, instructional improvement, the resolution of organizational and human development problems, and the faculty members' ability to move forward collectively depend on establishing effective communication among coworkers" (p. 1). Open lines of communication are established when the principal assumes a strong lead in manipulating time so that teachers have the opportunity to explore their own learning. Lack of communication impedes the synergy needed for growth. Joyce and Calhoun (1996) assert that:

> *as an entire faculty* [time] is central…Schoolwide change requires time for all members of the organization to work and study together. Without this collective study time, we cannot move forward as a learning community, only as individual 'points of light.'" (p. 181, emphasis in the original)

OPENING LINES OF COMMUNICATION: SOME PRACTICAL IDEAS

The principal can begin opening lines of communication by:

◆ Rethinking the use of support staff and itinerant teachers

Through creative utilization of substitutes, teachers can be released from duties before and during the school day.

♦ Utilizing blocks of time differently

Time during professional release and/or work days can be cleared of faculty meetings and other interruptions. If there is a need to meet during these types of work days, the effective principal has a well-prepared agenda so that faculty can continue working with one another on instructional issues.

♦ Modeling effective communication styles

The principal cannot expect to open lines of communication without a willingness to be available and to engage the community in learning. A mantra heard throughout schools is that the principal has an open-door policy. Although this policy is a good starting point, it is not enough to build a climate for opening communication channels. Effective principals open communication by acting as scouts (Calabrese & Zepeda, 1997), purposefully listening to and attaching meaning to what teachers have to say.

♦ Walking the walk

Principals need to be visible, to see first-hand what obstacles get in the way of teachers doing their jobs. Visibility diminishes in the main office.

♦ Providing emotional support

Teachers need to feel safe and secure—personally and professionally. Open inquiry and the changes that occur in teachers' practices as a result of staff development, need to be acknowledged by the principal. Because growth is the aim of staff development, teachers need emotional support to sustain the momentum to expand knowledge and refine skills.

♦ Enlisting the support of central office administrators

To further site-level initiatives and to secure resources, the principal communicates with central administrators to gain the support needed for success. Keeping central administrators informed also helps to minimize hearsay about activities occurring at the site. A community whose members can interact creates esprit de corps, or an enthusiasm for both the work and the people of the organization.

ELIMINATING TRADITIONAL SCHOOL BOUNDARIES

The astute principal observes how people are separated from one another and actively provides opportunities for all teachers to communicate with one another—across grade levels and subject areas—so that they can create a community of learners and not merely exist within predetermined "boundaries" (Morgan, 1986). Staff development linked to schoolwide improvement can also help the organization grow by eradicating traditional boundaries. By eliminating boundaries, teachers are more likely to see themselves and the organization growing together. When one part of the school does not know or understand how other parts work, then:

> Divisions tend to emphasize the distinctions between different elements of the organization, and to foster the development of political systems that place further barriers in the way of learning. The bounded rationality inherent in organizational design thus actually *creates* boundaries! Moreover, employees are usually encouraged to occupy and keep a predefined place within the whole, and are rewarded for doing so. (Morgan, 1986, p. 89, emphasis in the original)

The following Notes From the Field illustrates what effective principals can do to eliminate and/or flatten boundaries.

NOTES FROM THE FIELD: NEGOTIATING BOUNDARIES

Gary Elmen, principal of Waubonsie Valley High School (Naperville, Illinois, District 204) is responsible for the professional growth of over 200 teachers (1996-97 student enrollment was 2,940). Elmen believes that he was able to reduce isolation and build community within such a supersized high school by utilizing these strategies:

♦ Expanding the Role of the Department Chairs

   Department chairs work to hold frequent meetings with as many as 30 teachers. Department chairs meet biweekly with the administrative team (principal, assistant principals, deans, and guidance personnel). Elmen spends time and energy providing staff development for department chairs. This group attends retreats and workshops that build their capacity for leadership within the school. Department chairs have identified grade and subject area specialists who meet regularly with grade level and subject area colleagues. These coordinators rotate periodically so that more teachers can be involved in meaningful leadership positions.

♦ Focusing the Vision

   Teachers whose instructional strategies and activities reinforce the school's vision statement are honored with plaques at every faculty meeting. The principal describes the practice a supervisor has observed. Those teachers share later with interested colleagues. Similar awards are given for implementing cutting-edge technology that Waubonsie Valley has acquired.

♦ Celebrating Successes

   At every faculty meeting, Elmen and the administrative team "mug a teacher" to celebrate accomplishments. Peers nominate one another for "doing something good for the organization" no matter how big or small. One teacher received the symbolic coffee mug because of the way he diffused a potentially explosive parent and another teacher was "mugged" when she finished her masters degree.

◆ Forming Special Interest Groups that Tap into the Expertise of People

Waubonsie Valley High School (WVHS) hires between 25 and 50 teachers each year because of the rapid growth within the community it serves. Early on Elmen recognized that the administrative team alone could not provide the necessary induction, mentoring, and staff development activities. They created a culture that supported teachers who were in their first three years of teaching. Elmen used research on induction, mentoring, and available data about teacher retention to assist with framing the program. He used this information, coupled with three or four faculty members who were interested in these areas, to begin an ongoing and supportive mentoring program. The administration provides support, encouragement, and the needed resources. Through ongoing evaluation and monitoring, Elmen and the faculty at Waubonsie Valley High School make modifications to this program as the needs of the faculty change.

◆ Modeling

The administrative team models appropriate learning behaviors by participating in staff development activities as equals with teachers. The days of the principal beginning the activity and ducking out the back to door to "take an important call" are gone.

> Elmen's leadership has created teams of professional men and women working together. He has set the conditions so that the organizational structure of the school, despite its size, supports people working with one another. Clusters of colleagues in teams make this large school seem smaller.

Baloche (1998) suggests that principals:

- Believe, from the beginning, that people have the potential and desire to succeed; then support them.
- Build on a person's strengths.
- Provide their staff with feedback—encouragement, praise, and positive criticism—to help them grow.
- Build team spirit through retreats, cooperative efforts, and brainstorming sessions.
- Set high standards and praise the results; teachers will be proud of their organization.
- Remove obstacles to teachers' success by providing the necessary resources.
- Encourage teachers to take risks, to step out and try something new.
- Make work exciting with a relaxed, positive attitude.
- Let people see the results of their work praised.
- Listen carefully (pp. 239–249)

This view of leadership is empowering for teachers and for the organization. Leaders like Elmen have learned the lesson that "...principals are 'leaders of leaders' rather than sole leaders in the school and that they are both leaders and followers in ways that are critical to the accomplishment of the school's purpose...Principals can develop a leadership role that is both relevant and realistic" (Crow, Matthews, & Mc-Cleary, 1996, p. 44).

SUMMARY

This chapter provided an overview of the characteristics of principals as instructional leaders and of their role in staff development. Effectiveness in school leadership is characterized by an orientation toward continuous learning and tailored to the school's context. Any attempt to enrich the professional performance of teachers is classifiable as staff development. The degree to which initiatives are meaningful events or meaningless ventures is dependent on how they are supported by the principal (Rutherford, 1989).

A CASE STUDY FROM THE FIELD

Modeling Leadership
Jackson Elementary School
Dr. Dottie Caldwell, Principal
520 S. Wylie Road
Norman, OK 73069
405-366-5884
e-mail: dottiec@norman.k12.ok.us

CONTEXT

For the Norman Public Schools, professional development is expected as an integral part of each staff member's professional responsibility. Our district model for school improvement, *Decisions for Excellence,* is based on research that demonstrates that the most effective decision-making in the K-12 arena is site-based. District resources support all local site initiatives. Jackson Elementary is a K-5 school located in a suburban middle class neighborhood that serves a diverse population of approximately 400 students.

My role as principal is to empower my teaching staff to take responsibility not only for student learning, but for their own learning as well. When I first arrived, Jackson was a very traditional school. Top-down management and teacher-directed learning formed the foundation of operations at Jackson. Teachers were essentially independent operators.

Collaboration had to start with me; however, simply articulating my beliefs was not enough. My teachers needed to see my beliefs about teaching in action.

PROCESS

Transforming Jackson Elementary School into a thriving learning community required first building a team. My teachers needed to "see" that I was "one of them." My first step was to request volunteers who would agree to team-teach with me. I taught appreciation of literature in reading classes and enrichment activities in math classes. This practical demonstration was a more effective communication of my beliefs than any speech I could possibly have written. Teachers at Jackson began to take notice. While I had taken an important first step in facilitating team-building, there was still much work to be done.

I discovered that very few of our faculty members knew each other's families. The solution was simple: we had a party. Staff members who had worked side-by-side for 15 years were now, for the first time, forging social connections. As teachers became more comfortable with each other, conversation began to be transformed into meaningful dialogue concerning professional practice. To further this new effort toward collaboration, we instituted voluntary study groups to investigate existing literature on school improvement. Meaningful exchanges concerning curriculum, student learning, and needed professional development initiatives began to emerge. In addition to traditional in-service programming, we formed peer coaching and study groups to help each other.

We reserve one day each year for long-term planning and goal-setting. We share our goals and come to consensus on our theme for the upcoming year. The trust that we have built through collaborative learning has allowed to us not only celebrate our successes, but also to honestly assess our less successful ventures. We have learned to view obstacles as *opportunities.*

RESULTS

Our professional growth initiatives at Jackson Elementary have created a thriving learning community. Our focus community is clear: "Is it in the best interests of the children?" Each year, teachers set individual goals and collectively set three site goals. All stakeholders in our learning organization have played important roles in achieving our success.

Faculty meetings have become inadequate for sharing the learning that takes place in our community. For this reason, we have instituted the Friday Assembly for sharing learning. Each week, a different class shares its learning in creative ways: skits, reports, videotapes, and so forth. In addition, each year we host an evening of student-led presentations called Portfolio Evening. This event, held about three-fourths into the school year, is a celebration of all that our students have accomplished.

One specific goal of our teachers is the creation of an outdoor classroom. A parent, who is a landscape architect, volunteered design and building services for this project. Our dream of an outdoor classroom is now a reality. A second goal, integrating use of the Internet in our learning, is improving computer literacy of teachers and students alike.

As a result of new learning in faculty study groups, we determined that our existing grade report forms were not consistent with our beliefs concerning student assessment. Information important to parents could not be reported using the district provided forms. We received permission to pilot an experimental nongraded reporting form. The departure from traditional grade reporting caused an uproar from various stakeholders. After meeting with parents, teachers, and school-board members, we began using both the traditional graded reports and the nongraded assessment reports.

The learning community at Jackson Elementary School is a stronger organization because everyone is both leader and follower. All stakeholders are a part of the process. We are life-long learners who support creative teaching practice. We followup learning and implementation with data-driven results to modify changes in practice. All members of the Jackson learning community are encouraged to be innovative. A school tends to take on the personality of its leaders: its teachers and administrators. My role is as the catalyst. I have to set the example by being an active learner.

QUESTIONS

APPLICATION OF STAFF DEVELOPMENT PRINCIPLES

+ Based on your experience, what characteristics and behaviors typify instructional leaders? Examine your own leadership style and behavior. What did you discover about your leadership style? Based on your insight, what can you do to improve staff development in relation to your leadership style, behavior, and characteristics?

ACTION RESEARCH

+ Examine the communication patterns in your building. Collect artifacts (memos, agendas, and other printed items). Does this communication pattern empower teachers? Is this pattern reflected in staff development activities at your site?

PUTTING STAFF DEVELOPMENT INTO A CONTEXT

+ Develop a plan for involving teachers in the design and implementation of staff development for the upcoming school year. Focus attention on how you are going to build momentum for active involvement and teacher leadership.

SUGGESTED READINGS

Ackerman, R.H., Donaldson, G.A., & van der Bogert, R. (1996). *Making sense as a school leader: Persisting questions, creative opportunities.* San Francisco, CA: Jossey-Bass Publishers.

Blase, J., & Blase, J. (1998). *Handbook of instructional leadership: How really good principals promote teaching and learning.* Thousand Oaks, CA: Corwin Press.

Crow, G.M., Matthews, L.J., & McCleary, L.E. (1996). *Leadership: A relevant and realistic role for principals.* Larchmont, NY: Eye on Education.

McCall, J. (1997). *The principal as steward.* Larchmont, NY: Eye on Education.

Sergiovanni, T.J. (1992). *Moral leadership: Getting to the heart of school improvement.* San Francisco, CA: Jossey-Bass Publishers.

3

ADULTS LEARNING: RELEASING THE CONDITIONS FOR PROFESSIONAL GROWTH

Learning is not attained by chance, it must be sought for with ardor and attended to with diligence.

Abigail Adams

The cornerstone of successful staff development is the way in which adults are engaged in learning. Greene (1988) wrote:

> The aim is to find (or create) an authentic public space, one in which diverse beings can appear before one another as the best they know how to be. Such a space requires the provision of opportunities for the articulation of multiple perspectives in multiple idioms, out of which *something common can be brought into being.* (p. xi, emphasis in the original)

Greene's message is clear—adults need and want to grow professionally; they desire ongoing learning opportunities in a forum nestled within their own schools so that they can improve practice.

Reflect on the ways in which traditional staff development initiatives are designed and then offered. Typically, activities are launched in flurries at the beginning of the year, or they are offered as a means for teachers to earn "points" toward requirements for district accountability measures. Disconnected from site or district initiatives, staff development activities scheduled as one-shot events have little lasting impact on adults and their learning, and even more negligible effect on student learning, a tightly coupled goal of staff development. Providing learning opportunities for teachers and staff to grow—professionally and personally—are fundamental goals of staff development. For the principal to assist teachers with their growth, they need to explore the attributes of adult learning. These attributes should be incorporated into all staff development initiatives, regardless of the format, process, or content.

CHAPTER OBJECTIVES

♦ Examine the principles of adult learning—andragogy.
♦ Apply the principles of adult learning to staff development conditions.
♦ Recognize the continuum of career stages between beginning teachers, midcareer teachers, and career teachers.

ANDRAGOGY

Andragogy, an important concept in planning for staff development, has been defined as "the art and science of helping adults learn" (Knowles, 1970, p. 38). Understanding what motivates adults to grow enhances professional staff development, and helps the school to become a community of learners.

Principals, more often than not, come from the rank and file of the classroom. As former teachers, principals might have difficulty shifting their view of learning—they are no longer classroom teachers responsible for the learning activities of children. The principal now shifts his or her attention to the ways in which adults learn. This shift might be tumultuous in that principals often find their doorways littered with the problem children, who absorb a great deal of their time and energy. Absent too frequently are discussions about instruction, curriculum, staff development, and other topics that enhance adult and student learning. "Consequently, teachers and others in schools become preoccupied with the adult-child relationship at the expense of the potential power of the adult-adult relations." (Griffin, 1983, p. 236). Dalellew and Martinez (1988) provide an excellent overview of the differences in the ways in which children and adults learn. They indicate:

+ Adult-learning is more "self-directed" and…that …the impetus for learning is to share information, to generate one's own need for learning;

+ Adults seek knowledge that applies to their current life situation; they want to know how this new information will help them in their development;

+ Life experiences…shape their readiness for learning;

+ Adults have differing levels of readiness to learn; and,

+ Staff who voluntarily attend in-services, workshops, and seminars usually are those who have determined that they want to learn more. (pp. 28–29)

Joyce and McKibbin (1982) believe that teachers experience "growth states" where behaviors are labeled as *omnivores/active consumers, passive consumers, resistant,* and *withdrawn*. The following describe each one of these growth states:

+ Omnivores/Active Consumers

Adults who are omnivorous/active consumers participate actively in staff development activities; they thrive on learning more skills or refining existing ones; they are willing to experiment with what they have learned in *their classrooms*; and, they see staff development as an extension of their professionalism.

◆ Passive Consumers

Adults who are passive consumers merely participate by attending staff development activities; they rarely soak-up new knowledge or put new skills to use.

◆ Resistant

Adults who are resistant to staff development attend activities under informal and formal protests that are clearly articulated in the faculty lounge, halls, and principal's office. The resistant adult adamantly refuses, publicly and privately, to apply what is learned. There are many factors that can contribute to a resistant stance. Change or even the thought of change can strike fear in many people. Philosophical differences about a particular method or teaching strategy can engage people in resistant behaviors.

◆ Withdrawn

Withdrawn adults completely shut down and rarely attend staff development activities; they frequently arrive late and/or leave early; they are apathetic about their work; and, they remove themselves—socially and emotionally—from participation.

Like children, no two adults learn in the same manner or at the same rate. To understand the ways in which adults learn, the principal needs to have an understanding of who is on their faculty and the experiences, expertise, and skills that each member of the learning community brings. Adults as learners have different learning needs. The ability of the principal to understand and apply the principles of adult learning will determine, to a large extent, the success of learning opportunities.

Principles of Adult Learning

Staff development activities need to appeal to adults and their unique learning needs. Much research has been conducted on the ways in which adults learn. Zemke and Zemke (1995) conclude from their studies that:

♦ As they mature, adults tend to prefer self-direction.

♦ Adults' experiences are a rich resource for learning. Adults learn more effectively through experiential techniques such as discussion or problem-solving than they do through more passive techniques.

♦ Adults are aware of specific learning needs generated by real-life events.

♦ Adults are competency-based learners, meaning that they want to learn a skill or acquire knowledge that they can apply pragmatically to their immediate circumstances. (p. 32)

Zemke and Zemke's (1995) findings are consistent with the principles of andragogy. They focus on successes that can be achieved by an organization that promotes the development of adults who can be self-directed and who apply problem-centered approaches to the issues faced on the job. Teachers as learners are essential because they:

> ...have been asked to assume new responsibilities and adopt new practices that are substantially different from traditional notions about what it means to be a teacher. Under these circumstances, teachers need time to be learners themselves—a truth that is rarely factored...and is quite likely an important variable in the dismal track record of educational change efforts over the past 30 years. (Adelman, Walking Eagle, & Hargreaves, 1997, p. 2)

With the teacher as the center of learning, ongoing administrative support needs to be embedded in learning goals to create momentum for growth. When organizational and individual learning goals are coupled, staff development has the capacity to transform the school into a learning organization. Fostering a unified vision for what learning can become, the principal can include the community—teachers, professional staff, support staff, students, and parents. When all are engaged as learners, the organization is more capable of growth. *A Nation Prepared* (1986) states: "Teachers must think for themselves if they are to help others think for themselves, [and] be able to act independently and collaborate with others, and render critical judgment" (p. 25).

SETTING THE TEMPO FOR STAFF DEVELOPMENT AND THE ADULT LEARNER

An organization promotes adult learning at the tempo set by the principal, and the relationships built between teachers, professional staff, and the administration. Before setting the tempo, however, the principal should become familiar with basic human needs. Figure 3.1 is a guide that provides perspective about human needs and their implications for framing staff development for adults.

By examining the needs of adult learners from a growth perspective, principals can provide more meaningful staff development opportunities. Often, staff development and supervision are viewed from a "deficit" perspective (Ponticell, 1997), or as a "rehabilitation model...[where]...an instructional specialist may make several followup visits and suggest a variety of specialized programs for the teacher..." (Dalellew & Martinez, 1988, p. 29). Another view is that staff development will provide "relief" "...to meet an immediate need within the organization" (Dalellew & Martinez, 1988, p. 29). When these views are assumed by those who initiate staff development activities, it is unlikely that teachers will experience growth. The cycle of deficit thinking or knee-jerk staff development perpetuates the commonly held view that much of staff development deals with fads that recycle every decade.

Brookfield's (1995) view of the adult learner provides a more optimistic outlook:

FIGURE 3.1. NEEDS AND STAFF DEVELOPMENT

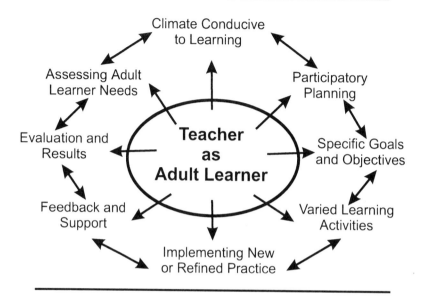

Viewing teachers as adult learners means that we focus on how they learn to make critically reflective judgements in the midst of action and how they change subsequent actions to take account of these insights. From the perspective of the adult learning tradition, assisting this uniquely adult form of learning becomes an important focus for any professional development activity. (p. 222)

UNRAVELING THE OBVIOUS: KNOW YOUR STAFF AS ADULT LEARNERS

Prior experiences are powerful sources of knowledge and should be considered as the principal is developing learning opportunities. Knowles (1992), cited by Brookfield (1995), indicates that "in any situation in which adults' experience is ignored or devalued, they perceive this as not just rejecting their experience, but rejecting them as persons" (p. 223). Knox (1977) believes that to appeal to the adult learner, opportunities for the active search for meaning need to be provided when new tasks are related to earlier activities.

Whether you are a new principal or have held the position for an extended time, it might be useful to profile the adult learners in your building. Figure 3.2 will help guide the principal in developing a profile of the faculty. With careful analysis, clues to the type of professional development activities (content and process) needed to meet individual and organizational goals can be discovered.

FIGURE 3.2. FACULTY PROFILE

Teacher	Years Experience	Highest Degree	Specialized Training
Adams	7	BS (Mathematics)	Cooperative learning applied to math
Bailey	15	MA + 15 Spanish & French	Spent 3 months in Spain

Such a profile can highlight experience and education; however, this type of profile does very little to provide insights about the developmental and professional stages of the faculty. This is a dilemma because adult needs can change over time as a result of experiences, professional development activities, and personal life events. Similar to young children, adults fluctuate in what they need, at any given time, in order to learn. However, if principals establish trusting relationships and build confidence, their teachers will reveal what they need. As a result, principals are in a better position to meet the learning needs of their teachers.

THE CONTINUUM OF TEACHER CAREER STAGES

To uncover career and/or developmental needs, the principal can model action research by engaging teachers in charting their own career stages (Newman, Burden, & Applegate, 1980). A caveat is offered, however: identifying the stages of teacher development is tricky business in that there are no absolutes. The astute principal makes a more informed guesstimate about stage development if the principal is familiar with general attributes of adult development and career stage theories.

Burden (1982) found in his research that changes occur over time in teacher's:

♦ Job skills, knowledge, and behaviors—in areas such as teaching methods, discipline strategies and curriculum planning;

♦ Attitudes and outlooks—in areas such as images of teaching, professional confidence and maturity, willingness to try new teaching methods, and concerns; and,

♦ Job events — in areas such as changes in grade level, school, or district; involvement in additional professional responsibilities; and age of entry and retirement. (pp. 1–2)

Burden's research further reveals that teachers go through three distinct stages: survival stage (first year of teaching), adjustment stage (years two through four), and mature stage (years five and beyond) (p. 2).

Earlier, Feiman and Floden (1980) discussed teacher growth in terms of career and developmental stages. Figure 3.3 depicts dominant ideas about teacher stages and career development. You are encouraged to think about your teachers while reviewing this figure. What you surmise from such an analysis might shed some insight on the staff development needs of teachers.

Newman, Burden, and Applegate (1980) developed a method to take the guesswork out of this process by having teachers identify their own career stage. Newman and her associates (1980) recommend that principals:

Have teachers draw a horizontal line across the blank page. This represents the time line of their teaching careers. Say, "Careers may be marked by different stages, experiences, changes. If you were to divide your teaching career into several parts, what would mark your divisions? Mark them down on the line. Jot down the special characteristics of each part." (p. 8)

FIGURE 3.3. CAREER STAGES AND DEVELOPMENTAL NEEDS

Stage	Name	Approximate Years in Field	Developmental Theory and Needs
1	Preservice	0	Training and preparation for a profession.
2	Formative Years	1–2	Survival Stage (Burden, 1982; Feiman & Floden, 1980). Seeks safety and desires to learn the day-to-day operations of the school and the complexities of facing new situations in the classroom. (Ponticell & Zepeda, 1996).
3	Building Years	3–5	Confidence in work mounts as does understanding. Building the multifaceted role of teaching.
4	Striving to Develop Professionally Years	5–8	Actively seeks out professional development and other opportunities for professional growth; high job satisfaction (Burke, Christensen, & Fessler, 1984, p. 15).
5	Crisis Periods	Varies	Teacher burnout (Burke, Christensen, & Fessler 1984, p. 15).
6	Complacency	Varies	Complacency sets in; innovation is low.
7	Career Wind-Down	Varies	Kahuna status lets the teacher get by without exerting much effort.
8	Career Exit	Varies	Retirement

Based on the work of Burden (1982); Burke, Christensen, and Fessler (1984); Christensen, Burke, Fessler, and Hagstrom (1983); Feiman and Floden (1980); Newman, Dornburg, Dubois, and Kranz (1980); and Ponticell and Zepeda (1996).

After teachers have self-identified where they are in their careers, the principal needs to provide a forum for sharing this private information.

NOTES FROM THE FIELD

Capitol Hill High School (Oklahoma City) principal Raul Font has devised a way to help his teachers to both identify their career stages and to set learning goals for the year. Mr. Font believes that teachers need to set goals across three levels—professional, personal, and academic—for students in their classrooms.

During the first month of school, Mr. Font meets with each teacher to discuss goals for the academic year. Figure 3.4 is the professional and personal goals worksheet used at Capitol Hill High School and is reproduced in part for you to consider. Mr. Font believes that goal-setting conferences have allowed him to know his teachers better and to open lines of communication. He also believes these conferences help put teachers at ease when discussing their career development. At the end of the year, Mr. Font meets individually with teachers so that they can discuss goal attainment or examine goal modification.

SUMMARY

Professional development is most effective "...when it fits into teachers' personal schedules" (Adelman, Walking Eagle, & Hargreaves, 1997, p. 57). The principal has to actively seek ways to eliminate barriers to teachers finding the time and resources to improve their practices (Cross, 1981). Adult learning needs can be met with staff development that focuses on growth, is practical, and relates directly to the individual interests and needs of teachers. Darling-Hammond and Goodwin (1993) state: "...The strength and legitimacy of any profession depends on the continued growth and development of its members...Professional organizations must have effective mechanisms that provide opportunity for consultation,

FIGURE 3.4. PROFESSIONAL AND PERSONAL GOALS WORKSHEET

Capitol Hill High School
1998-99 PROFESSIONAL/PERSONAL GOALS

Professional Goal:

_____

_____

_____

Objectives for Goal:

A. _____

_____

B. _____

_____

Personal Goal:

_____

_____

_____

Objectives for Goal

A. _____

_____

B. _____

_____

Academic Goal:

_____

_____

Objectives for Goal:

A. _____

_____

B. _____

_____

_____

Signature   Date   Print Name

reflection, self-assessment, and continued improvement" (p. 42).

Langenbach (1993) believes that adults need to take initiative for their own learning by:

> ...capitalizing on life experiences...Replacing the notion that learning has to be associated with an educational institution with the realization that learning can and does take place all the time in and out of organizations...(p. 165)

There is no more powerful method for principals to communicate this axiom to teachers than by modeling a proactive learning posture. Principals who are active learners have taken the first step in creating a community of learners.

A CASE STUDY FROM THE FIELD

Mentoring Program
Amarillo Independent School District
Sandy Whitlow, Coordinator
Amarillo Independent School District Support Center
7200 I-40 West
Amarillo, TX 79106
(806)-354-4772

THE DISTRICT

Amarillo (population approximately 158,000) is in the Texas panhandle, open-range cattle country once known as the *Llano Estacado* (staked plains). The school district serves about 30,000 students, 48% of whom are classified as economically disadvantaged. About 35% of the district's teachers have less than 5 years experience. Since fall 1992 the school district has developed, implemented, and refined a mentor program to address the needs of its beginning teachers.

THE MENTOR INITIATIVE

While the Texas Education Agency mandates that each first-year teacher be assigned a mentor, the mandate neither requires nor provides for mentor training. Thus, it is not uncommon for a first-year teacher and mentor to have little knowledge about mentoring and little structure or process to guide the process. To address this problem, the Amarillo Independent School District (AISD) has worked with Dr. Leslie Huling of Southwest Texas State University and Dr. Judith Ponticell of Texas Tech University to develop a research-based mentor program. Dr. Huling provided training in stages of concern and mentoring styles in 1992 and 1993. Since 1994 Dr. Ponticell has provided training in the professional development of beginning teachers; developmental approaches to mentoring; videotaping and conferencing approaches; problem-solving approaches; needs assessment; and program evaluation.

MENTOR PROGRAM OBJECTIVES

The goals of the AISD Mentor Program are:

♦ To improve beginning teachers' instructional performance;

♦ To increase beginning teacher retention;

♦ To promote beginning teachers' personal and professional well-being; and,

♦ To develop beginning teachers' understanding of the culture of the school system.

PROGRAM COMPONENTS

Experienced teachers interested in being mentors volunteer for the program. Individuals who enter into the district's mentor pool must have at least three years teaching experience in AISD and be rated as excellent or exceeding expectations by their principals. Mentors are eligible for a $150 stipend. Mentors attend a one-day training session at the beginning of the school year and a half-day support session each semester. Training includes perspectives on the problems and development of beginning teachers, stages of concern, developmental approaches to mentoring, videotaping and conferencing approaches, and problem-solving approaches.

Every beginning teacher in AISD is paired with a mentor. When mentors are assigned, every attempt is made to provide the beginning teacher with a mentor who is at the same school. If a mentor must be assigned from another school, the school is in close proximity. A principal may also request a mentor for any teacher who is experienced but new to the district or who is returning to the district after an absence of two years or more.

In addition to the initial training day, the school district provides for two half-days per semester for the mentor to observe the beginning teacher's classroom and conference about the observation and for the beginning teacher to visit the mentor's classroom. Between these formal sessions, the mentor and beginning teacher use videotaping and/or after-school problem-solving conferences to address immediate classroom concerns.

A half-day sharing and support session is also provided by the district each semester. Mentors meet with other mentors to talk about their experiences, receive support from the trainer or support center personnel and engage in collegial problem solving. Beginning teachers meet with other beginning teachers to talk about their concerns in the classroom and their mentoring experiences. Information gathered at these sessions assists support center personnel in identifying additional staff development needs or programmatic needs. At the end of the year, the beginning teacher and the mentor evaluate the mentor pairing and the mentor program as a whole.

An important component of the AISD Mentor Program is the no-fault opportunity for a mentoring pair to dissolve the pairing. In the event that one or both of the parties in a mentoring pair cannot establish a satisfying professional working relationship, the pairing may be dissolved by mutual agreement and/or can be facilitated by the principal or program coordinator and a new pairing is established. We believe that it is imperative that this option be exercised when necessary and that the dissolution is not viewed as a failure on the part of either individual.

EFFECTS OF THE MENTOR PROGRAM

The AISD Mentor Program began its seventh year in fall 1998. Both training and program evaluations over the past six years indicate that the retention rate of beginning teachers has improved. Appraisals of beginning teachers indicate increased classroom effectiveness. Mentors consistently report gains in confidence and competence in providing assistance to beginning teachers and in helping beginning teachers to become better problem solvers. It was important to the mentors that they saw the beginning teachers gain independence and increase their self-efficacy. Beginning teachers consistently report increased motivation to remain in teaching, increased confidence in solving classroom problems, and increased feelings of support and belonging in the school district.

SUPPORT OF THE MENTOR PROGRAM

The AISD school board, district administration, and principals have made a commitment to support this program. Money for mentor stipends, training, and release time for observation/conferencing days, and support session days are built into the district's staff development budget.

The workload of mentor and beginning teachers increases. Both, however, indicate that the time they allocate to meeting regularly and participating in the required program components are professionally satisfying and worthwhile. The state's new Professional Development and Appraisal System, which began implementation in fall 1998, contains a goal-setting and self-evaluation component. Both mentors and beginning teachers who have participated in the Mentor Program thus far, see important connections between the work of a mentor pair and the appraisal system.

IN SUMMARY

The development of a successful beginning teacher is not the responsibility of colleges and university teacher education programs alone, nor will state mandates alone improve beginning teachers' experiences in their first schools and school districts. The AISD Mentor Program has made a long-term commitment to allocate the money and resources necessary to turn an education and a mandate into a workable support system that increases the likelihood of a beginning teacher's success in AISD. That success ultimately develops stronger teachers for our children.

QUESTIONS

APPLICATION OF STAFF DEVELOPMENT PRINCIPLES

♦ Why is the knowledge about adult learning theory, motivation theory, and staff development essential in planning and designing professional growth opportunities?

♦ Should staff development activities be the same for all teachers? Respond.

ACTION RESEARCH

♦ Visit a school that has a mentoring program for newly-hired teachers. Identify the principles of adult learning that guide the support given to newly-hired teachers.

♦ Design a questionnaire to determine the needs of the adult learners in the building in which you work. What types of information would you need to gather? What could you do in your current situation to incorporate what you have learned?

PUTTING STAFF DEVELOPMENT INTO A CONTEXT

♦ Examine your beliefs about adult learning and the way that you personally prefer to learn new information. Now think about the absolutely best staff development activities in which you participated. How did these activities speak to the adult learner in you?

SUGGESTED READINGS

Adelman, N.E., Walking Eagle, K.P., & Hargreaves, A. (1997). *Racing with the clock: Making time for teaching and learning in school reform.* New York, NY: Teachers College Press.

Brookfield, S.D. (1995). *Becoming a critically reflective teacher.* San Francisco, CA: Jossey-Bass Publishers.

Langenbach, M. (1993). *Curriculum models of adult education.* Malabar, FL: Krieger Publishing Company.

Richey, R. (1992). *Designing instruction for the adult learner: Systematic training theory and practice.* London: Kogan Page Limited.

4

DEVELOPING LEARNING COMMUNITIES FOR ADULTS

The degree to which I create relationships which facilitate growth of others as separate persons is a measure of the growth I have achieved in myself.

Carl Rogers

A premise of this book is that schools can become learning communities if the principal is willing to launch the potential of his or her people. This is necessary because "…principals must intimately be involved in the instructional life of their schools. Through that involvement, they can provide the leadership essential to the school's success as a learning center" (Ackerman, Donaldson, & van der Bogert, 1996, pp. 31–32). As schools become more complex, there is a need to begin reconceptualizing the ways in which adults work with one another so that they can "…act wisely and feel deeply, within an environment that challenges the individual to look beyond her/himself and [to] experience the value of interdependence" (O'Reilly & Latimer, 1990, p. 1).

A learning community is built by everyone in the organization. It will only evolve if the leader actively nurtures and models growth-oriented practices and processes. As the leader of a learning community, a principal should possess a strong resolve to create and sustain the conditions needed to build capacity in the individual and the organization. Finally, the role of the principal in a learning community needs to change *from* that of telling teachers how to teach and selling teachers on new fads *to* that of facilitating the processes by which teachers can discover knowledge about themselves and their practices.

This chapter examines the development of the school as a learning organization, committed to bringing together the individual talents of teachers into a collective, powerful, and synergistic force to reflect on their practices. The only way to develop "a good school and a healthy workplace is [through] community" (Barth, cited in O'Reilly & Latimer, 1990, p. 1). From these premises, we begin our journey through learning communities.

CHAPTER OBJECTIVES

+ Explore what we know about learning communities.

+ Highlight the characteristics of successful learning communities.

+ Examine how principals can support the development of a learning community.

WHAT WE KNOW ABOUT LEARNING COMMUNITIES

A learning community is a group of individuals who share a similar vision of educational values and beliefs (e.g., honesty, respect, trust, courage, and compassion). As a result of this shared vision, a community of learners can work toward common goals that enhance professional and personal development. In addition, a community of learners, whose work and activities are linked to the organization, helps the organization grow. Through collaborative efforts, a community of learners creates synergy, a synchronized energy where the power of the group is more profound than that of any one individual. Covey (1992) indicates that "…the whole is more than the sum of the parts" (p. 37). Sergiovanni (1994) offers that:

> Community is the tie that binds students and teachers together in special ways, to something more significant than themselves: shared values

and ideals. It lifts both teachers and students to higher levels of self-understanding, commitment, and performance—beyond the reaches of the shortcomings and difficulties they face in their everyday lives...with a unique and enduring sense of identity, belonging, and place. (p. xiii)

Senge defines a learning community as "an organization in which people at all levels are, collectively, continually enhancing their capacity to create things they really want to create" (O'Neil, 1995, p. 20). In *The Fifth Discipline*, Senge (1990) introduces the idea of the learning organization:

where people continually expand their capacity to create the results they truly desire, where new and expansive patterns of thinking are nurtured, where collective aspiration is set free, and where people are continually learning how to learn together. (p. 3)

Sergiovanni (1994) believes that "community can help teachers and students be transformed from a collection of 'I's' to a collective 'we,' thus providing...a unique and enduring sense of identity, belonging, and place" (p. xiii).

While traditional staff development approaches to learning have focused on helping educators hone individual skills, learning involves the collective capacity of all people in the organization. According to O'Neil (1995), Senge maintains that learning in education, like business, "involves fundamental cultural changes" (p. 21). This requires collective reflection regarding the creation of significant and enduring initiatives and behaviors which result in accomplishment. O'Neil (1995) adds, however, that creating a learning community is a difficult venture within the education system, because of the fragmented way in which schools are organized (e.g., departments, grade levels, and specialty groups such as gifted and talented).

LEADERSHIP PRACTICES THAT SUSTAIN LEARNING

A community needs a clear *focus* to sustain learning and to keep everyone moving in the same direction. The needs of individuals and the organization must be identified so that stakeholders can embrace learning itself for its *intrinsic rewards*. In learning communities, those closest to making the school successful have had a voice in developing, implementing, and evaluating staff development initiatives. If the principal wants to transform instruction and learning, the principal should first examine *core beliefs* about staff development as a vehicle to improve "what's best for kids." This exploration cannot be done in isolation. A major tenet in learning communities is that an *interconnectedness* exists among members of the community. In the case of instruction and its continued improvement, Goodlad (1979) states:

> It is entirely reasonable to expect every teacher to develop and use a guiding framework of concepts, principles, and methods that appear to influence the learning process positively. Since our knowledge of what is likely to be productive is increasing, it behooves every teacher to take responsibility for continued professional growth. And it should go without saying that the school district, as employer, has sufficient stake in this professional growth to provide staff development programs geared to the demands and needs of classroom teaching—not to the pet projects of administrators or school board members. (pp. 91–92)

THE CHANGING ROLES OF AUTHORITY IN LEARNING ORGANIZATIONS

To provide the conditions that support learning communities, a broader picture of the school is needed. This broader picture includes examining the role of teachers and others, including the principal, and the ways in which decisions are made. Sergiovanni (1996) believes that leaders, "plant the seeds of community...They lead by following. They lead by service...[and] by involving others to share in the burdens of leadership" (p. xix). Similarly, Senge (1996) indicates that leaders who want to promote a learning organization are "seed carriers" who "connect people of like mind in diverse settings to each other's learning efforts" (pp. 55–56).

Leaders in a learning community come from within the rank and file of teachers and professional staff who work alongside the principal. Forest (1998) states: "There are no real short cuts to building community thoroughly from the ground up and maintaining it vigilantly over time. Basic to this understanding is the realization that community grows from within. It can be fostered from without—indeed it must be to survive—but it cannot be imposed" (p. 291).

TEACHER DEVELOPMENT: THE HEART OF A LEARNING ORGANIZATION

We can build a learning community by reconceptualizing how we think about teacher and organizational development through an examination of processes and practices that:

- Encourage teachers to reflect on their own practice;
- Acknowledge that teachers develop at different rates, and that at any given time some teachers are more ready to learn new things than others;
- Acknowledge that teachers have different talents and interests;
- Give high priority to conversation...among teachers;
- Provide for collaborative learning among teachers;
- Emphasize caring relationships and felt interdependencies;
- Call upon teachers to respond morally to their work; and,
- View teachers as supervisors of learning communities. (Sergiovanni, 1996, p. 142)

RELEASING THE CONDITIONS OF GROWTH

Sergiovanni's (1996) enlightened view of the centrality of the teacher as learner promotes reflection and collaborative relationships that can help meet the needs of both the organization and its people—all the while building capacity:

> All organizations learn, but not always for the better. A learning organization is an organization that has an enhanced capacity to learn, adapt, and change. It is an organization in which learning processes are analyzed, monitored, developed, managed, and aligned with improvement and innovation goals. (Gephart et al., 1996, p. 36)

From examining what we know about learning communities, it is clear that building one takes all the members of the organization working toward common values and goals. No longer is the administrator merely a leader, nor is the role of teacher solely that of follower. Each assumes these responsibilities equally (see, for example, Gephart et al., 1996; Senge, 1996; Sergiovanni, 1996).

CHARACTERISTICS OF LEARNING COMMUNITIES

Significant research, especially that of Senge and Sergiovanni, has contributed to the growing knowledge and understanding of learning communities. For the organization, profit is important, but so, too, is the professional enhancement of employees. In schools, profit is threefold:

- ◆ The development of teachers (refining existing skills, learning new skills, and keeping abreast with new and emerging knowledge within subject areas);
- ◆ The enhancement of student learning as a result of such efforts; and,
- ◆ The empowerment of teachers who can model life-long learning to students.

LEARNING COMMUNITIES ARE CHARACTERIZED BY INCLUSIVE ENVIRONMENTS

In a community of learners, the principal creates an inclusive environment for both students and teachers. Brookfield (1986) indicates that "when adults teach and learn in one another's company, they find themselves engaging in a challenging, passionate, and creative activity" (p. 1). An inclusive environment fosters ongoing dialogue among its participants. Teachers are free to discuss issues, regardless of the topic. These ideas are consistent with Starratt's (1996) view of a learning community, where collective meaning is embraced daily through open discussion and reflection among the members of the community.

LEARNING COMMUNITIES SUPPORT CHANGE

The changes that schools have undergone throughout history are complex. To develop a learning community, the principal must begin by examining the complexities associated with power. In the view expressed by Senge et al. (1994), leaders who want to create a learning organization give up power and assume a mind-set that "no power is power" (p. 55). The structure of the organization and the leadership style of the principal needs to support the development of a learning community and the changes that will occur. Authentic change comes from individuals working toward a common goal.

Change from a personal perspective needs to be understood if the principal is to move the school organization toward forming a learning community. With understanding, staff development, supervision, and other forms of collegial support, changes in practice can be made.

NOTES FROM THE FIELD

Principal Raul Font (Capitol Hill High School, Oklahoma City) builds the staff development program by surveying the needs of teachers. The Staff Development Committee analyzes results and begins planning for the upcoming year. Figure 4.1 is a sample survey.

FIGURE 4.1. SAMPLE STAFF SURVEY

Capitol Hill High School
1998-99 Staff Development Suggestions

Please mark the suggested staff development topics you are interested in for the 1998-99 school year. Feel free to add any topic(s) you deem necessary, as well as possible speakers.

Name:_____ Date:_____ Position:_____

# *in order of* *choice*	*Topic*
	Service Learning
	Learning Styles
	Parent Involvement
	Assertive Discipline
	Classroom Management
	Curriculum Alignment
	Cooperative Learning
	Content Area Instruction for ESL Students
	Incorporating "Learner Outcomes" in your Daily Lesson plans
	Time-On-Task
	Portfolio Evaluation and Assessment
	Enhancing Students' Writing/Reading Skills
	Behavior Modification
	Democratic Schools' Research
	Developing Leadership Skills
	Increasing Self-Esteem
	Classroom Intervention
	Effective Schools Research
	Higher-Order Thinking Skills
	Exchange Program (Instructional/Administrative)
	Gangs

By adapting inclusiveness, the principal can minimize the stress associated with change. You are encouraged to refer to Chapter 7 for a more in-depth discussion of change and its effects on staff development.

LEARNING COMMUNITIES ARE COLLABORATIVE

Through collaboration, the power to make a difference is shared by all the members of the community. As early as 1979, Goodlad indicated that the learning community "…requires a collaborative effort, with less hand-wringing about imposed restraints, and less looking for someone else to blame, at least before we have exerted maximum effort to fulfill our own personal responsibilities" (p. 81). Teachers are willing to take risks in an environment that encourages (without facing retribution for less than satisfactory progress) efforts at hitting the target. Through collaboration, the climate of a learning community moves from being a frozen tundra to a warm, supportive haven for the generation of new, diverse ideas and practices.

LEARNING COMMUNITIES SUPPORT AUTONOMY AND FOSTER CONNECTEDNESS AMONG MEMBERS

There is a natural tension between autonomy and connectedness. People thrive in communities that nurture independence and free-thinking individuals who can join together to express values and beliefs. However, there is a need for people to feel bound by a common vision about learning. Effective principals reconcile the tensions between autonomy and interconnectedness by:

♦ Accepting people in a nonjudgmental manner;

♦ Promoting a willingness in others to listen and share ideas; and,

♦ "Lighting fires" by valuing growth and finding relevance in the work teachers do.

LEARNING COMMUNITIES
PROMOTE A COMMON VISION

Reitzug and Burello (1995) found that principals helped teachers..."clarify personal visions which ultimately strengthen the organizational vision" (p. 49), a key component of organizational learning. Senge and his associates (1994) indicate that "...the discipline of building shared vision is centered around a never-ending process, whereby people in an organization articulate vision, purpose, values, why their work matters, and how it fits in the larger world" (p. 298). Vision is powerful when the principal creates:

> ...ongoing processes in which people at every level of the organization, in every role, can speak from the heart about what really matters to them and be heard....The quality of this process...determines the quality and the power of the results. (Senge et al., 1994, p. 299)

To "hear" the voice of the community, the principal needs to involve all stakeholders—teachers, students, parents, staff (e.g., secretaries, maintenance persons, and cafeteria workers), central administrators, and members of the broader community the school serves (e.g., the neighborhood and the local business sector)—in the process of developing the school's vision. All views need to be considered in an apolitical forum.

WORK WITH TEACHERS TO CREATE THE VISION

With the principal's active involvement, barriers that might undermine the vision can be identified. Teachers are creative problem-solvers when they have an empowered voice. They can help the principal make changes within the operating structure of the school. Through ongoing refinement and removal of barriers, the right conditions bring the vision to life.

PROVIDE COORDINATION MECHANISMS

Most schools are large organizations where teachers work most of the day in isolation. Weekly faculty meetings are typically filled with agenda items that merely disseminate information. The effective principal uses this meeting time to facilitate discussion of important issues. Because it can be difficult to discuss critical issues in a large group setting, employ small groups, but report formulated ideas to the collective group for expanded discussion in order to be processed by all members of the learning community.

The principal can utilize mechanisms such as cooperative learning to commit small group ideas to writing. Often roles such as recorder, researcher, and timer are developed within groups that utilize cooperative learning. The principal can be sensitive by not assigning such roles, but by encouraging group members to develop roles for themselves. With the assistance of the school secretary, *artifacts* of the vision-building process can be produced. With results distributed in a timely manner, the principal can help sustain the creative momentum of the community.

MAINTAIN AND IMPROVE INTERPERSONAL SKILLS

Developing a collective vision, based on the beliefs, attitudes, and prior history of the school, can create tensions for community members. Divergent points of view need to be communicated so that all can reflect upon the meanings of these views. If an atmosphere of openness is created among the members, then divergent points of view can be examined in a nonthreatening manner. Interpersonal skills need to be nurtured to support a more responsive learning environment.

RECOGNIZE POLITICAL ALLEGIANCES

When all stakeholders are involved in the process of framing the school's vision, politics enters into the process. Without making a value judgment, many members bring their own agendas to the community. Depending on the *perceived* power of community members, allegiances can form, causing interests to splinter the whole into parts and further reinforcing hidden agendas. A learning community is able to overcome "part" thinking and behavior when members can agree upon common purposes that assist in creating a vision that can be embraced and infused into the daily operations of the school.

EXAMINE MOTIVATION

Members are motivated to develop a community vision that is relevant to individual and collective practices. Principals cannot force people to participate in the process. It is realistic to expect a third of the faculty to embrace the process, a third of the faculty to be initially neutral, and a third of the faculty to resist. This point of view might appear to be overly pessimistic; however, people only work hard when they are motivated. Some people are motivated by external factors and others by internal factors. Herzberg (1968) developed the motivator-hygiene theory that can be blended with Maslow's hierarchy of needs theory. By examining Herzberg's and Maslow's work in relation to motivation, the principal is better able to understand what motivates people. From this understanding, the principal is in a better position to nurture an environment that is more responsive to the needs of the community. Figure 4.2 illustrates Herzberg's and Maslow's theories.

SUMMARY

This chapter introduced the reader to the foundation on which successful staff development initiatives are built—a reflective, learning community. When a school is transformed into a learning community, all stakeholders are valued, collaboration is the norm, learning occurs naturally, and reflection is fostered through collegial conversations.

Because learning communities value persons as individuals, change no longer needs to be viewed as a threat to any stakeholder's worth. The implication is clear—the transformation of the school into a learning community must begin with the principal. The principal sets the tone for learning by modeling active learning, investing time in the process, and by empowering teachers as leaders.

FIGURE 4.2. UNDERSTANDING MOTIVATION

	Herzberg Motivation Model	*Maslow's Hierarchy of Needs*
High Order Needs		
Motivation	• Job content • Achievement • Recognition • Work itself • Responsibility • Growth • Advancement	• Need for Knowledge • Need for Understanding • Self-Actualization
Low Order Needs		
Hygiene Factors	• Pay/Salary • Fringe Benefits • Type of Supervision • Company Policies & Procedures • Status • Job Security • Interpersonal Relations	• Survival Needs • Security Needs • Belonging Needs • Esteem Needs

Adapted from Gage and Berliner, 1988; Jennings, 1993; and Razik and Swanson, 1995.

A CASE STUDY FROM THE FIELD

Cluster Groups
Eisenhower Elementary School
Patricia Simons, Principal
1415 Fairlawn
Norman, OK 73071
(405) 366-5879

CONTEXT

In January 1997, the faculty focused on Effective Schools research and processed "Where We Are" against the 12 most significant indicators. The five areas that the faculty decided to work on were tangible resources, reaching out to the knowledge base, experimentation, trust and confidence, and protection of what's important. In August 1997, the faculty produced action plans and time-lines. Possible strategies and potential roadblocks were identified.

Reviewing these data, the faculty established a Professional Development/School Improvement Committee for the 1997-98 school year to facilitate and promote a focus on reaching out to the knowledge base and experimentation. After surveying the faculty concerning coaching partners, it became obvious to faculty leaders that the current research and knowledge base in the areas of mentorship and reflective practice were not in place for coaching partners.

A university professor agreed to serve as an outside consultant. After brainstorming "what if?" lists, she proposed the idea of whole-faculty cluster groups to focus on staff-generated topics that would positively effect student learning. The consultant met with the principal and teacher leaders in a planning session a month prior to the workshop, to better understand the group's perspectives, purposes, and goals.

The consultant provided three hours of training, entitled "Creating Professional Development Clusters." Ten clusters were formed as part of the workshop and have been working together for the entire second semester. A Cluster Showcase was held a few months later for groups to share accomplishments, roadblocks, frustrations, and recommendations. These data will be used to make modifications in cluster groups to better meet the needs of faculty and to better impact student learning.

Initially, the consultant and the principal selected key teacher leaders to plan the Creating Professional Development Clusters workshop. The workshop was an outstanding success and enthusiasm was high as the groups began meeting and working. Some of the faculty were tentative about the concept because it was something very different. Everyone, at the outset, was willing to participate. Work during the semester had a mixed review: outstanding for some, problematic for others. Group feedback was generated and shared for individuals and groups to suggest modifications and/or changes that needed to be made. Faculty buy-in is a critical element for any initiative.

PROCESS

The goal of cluster groups is to provide a vehicle for colleagues to work together. Small groups focused on research-based practice and supported each other in risk taking. Research was presented that supported the mentoring process and demonstrated that professional growth does not occur in isolation. The consultant then asked the faculty to generate topics that positively effect student learning. Consensus was reached and staff selected their topics. Faculty meeting time was protected once a month for clusters to meet and work on goal areas. Additional monthly meeting time was an expectation. Teachers either requested other staff to cover classes or they met before or after school. Each cluster collaboratively established goals, action plans, and methods of documentation. They generated a list of resources and literature searches in each area and also supported each other in planning and implementing lessons with students.

Time is the key to any kind of professional development program where colleagues support each other in the change process. Teachers must have release time for joint learning opportunities. Time before and after school was seldom utilized because it was already reserved for so many other projects. Although district funding was available, resources within the site's budget were adequate to cover the initiative's costs.

Individual cluster group members networked with colleagues in other school districts. This program was shared with district administrators at a semi-annual presentation of site goals at the end of the year.

RESULTS

At the end of the initial semester of implementation the cluster concept was evaluated. Cluster groups provided a focus for the faculty on practices that have a direct impact on student learning. The heart of school improvement is the infusion of best practice into individual classrooms.

Cluster groups moved us light years ahead in faculty collaboration, and helped us focus on areas with potential for growth in student and adult learning. We learned that any new concept needs to be nurtured. Facilitators from within the faculty were trained to keep the clusters focused. We are now examining proactive strategies to encourage disinterested learners to participate.

Cluster groups made a difference in our school this year by introducing teachers to new strategies for planning quality lessons that motivate student learning.

QUESTIONS

APPLICATION OF STAFF DEVELOPMENT PRINCIPLES

- Based on this chapter (and others in this book), how can the development of a learning community promote professional development?

ACTION RESEARCH

- At your site, identify artifacts, programs, and activities that make the school a community. Explain the importance of each. If you had to make a presentation to the board of education, what would be most important to communicate about the community? Develop a 15- to 20-minute presentation on the school as a community utilizing technology (e.g., presentation software).

- Interview a cross-section of teachers, students, parents, local community members, and central administrators from your district. Ask them to describe the school as a learning community. What common items keep appearing across the sampling of people? What would you want to tell the superintendent about the perceptions of the school as a learning community?

PUTTING STAFF DEVELOPMENT INTO A CONTEXT

- ◆ Visit a school that you know absolutely nothing about and take a tour of the building. What did you discover about this school as a learning community?

- ◆ Identify the organizational barriers that impede your school site from becoming a learning community. What strategies need to be developed to address these barriers?

SUGGESTED READINGS

Evans, R. (1996). *The human side of school change: Reform, resistance, and the real-life problems of innovation.* San Francisco, CA: Jossey-Bass Publishers.

Sergiovanni, T.J. (1994). *Building community in schools.* San Francisco, CA: Jossey-Bass Publishers.

Starratt, R.J. (1996). *Transforming educational administration: Meaning, community, and excellence.* New York, NY: McGraw-Hill.

5

JOB-EMBEDDED LEARNING: A MORE EFFECTIVE STAFF DEVELOPMENT

Time takes all and gives all.
Giordano Bruno,
The Candle Bearer

One of the most difficult resources to manage, perhaps because of its brutally finite nature, is time. Time governs nearly every facet of America's schools. The school day, school year, and subject matter are all organized according to time. School subjects from the straightforward to the complex are assigned the same amount of time. School attendance, graduation requirements, state and locally mandated staff development requirements, and staff salaries are organized on the basis of time (McCall, 1997). To make the best possible use of time, priorities need to be set. Important tasks take precedence over insignificant ones. Time is an important resource for quality professional learning (Wood, Killian, McQuarrie, & Thompson, 1993).

In *First Things First*, Stephen Covey and his associates discuss at length "empowerment from the inside out" (Covey, Merrill, & Merrill, 1994, p. 238). Covey delineates three things necessary for empowerment from within to occur:

- Cultivate necessary conditions for empowerment,
- "Feast" on feedback, and
- Become a leader and servant (p. 239)

As in all professions, teachers need to be empowered to continue learning throughout their entire careers. According to research, staff development that is conducted as an integral part of the daily work routine is more effective than disjointed activities conducted as one-shot in-services throughout the school year. When staff development becomes a learning experience on a daily and ongoing basis, professional educators refer to this process as job-embedded staff development.

Job-embedded staff development can take many forms. Among these are mentoring, reflection, study groups, and peer coaching (including videotape analysis) (Sparks & Hirsh, 1997; Setteducati, 1995; Storeygard & Fox, 1995). The goals of job-embedded staff development are clearly delineated in the research: transfer and application of newly learned skills into classroom practice (Bennett, 1995; Wood & Killian, 1998), development of professionalism and collegiality (Ponticell, 1995), and school improvement (Wood & Killian, 1998). The major importance of job-embedded staff development models is their customized nature and immediate applicability for the learner. Mortenson and Grady (1979) state that "the value of job-embedded training lies in its unity with the teacher's job and the economy of accomplishing several purposes at once" (p. 4).

CHAPTER OBJECTIVES

- Define job-embedded staff development.
- Identify the attributes of job-embedded staff development.
- Identify the essential conditions for job-embedded staff development.
- Identify implications for principals as staff developers.

WHAT IS JOB-EMBEDDED STAFF DEVELOPMENT?

Job-embedded staff development is "learning that occurs as teachers and administrators engage in their daily work activities" (Wood & Killian, 1998, p. 52). For job-embedded models of staff development to be successful, active participation of school leaders at all levels within the local district is essential. Every person in the district—from the classroom teacher to the superintendent—becomes a leader as well as a learner if learning is job-embedded. Job-embedded staff development is replete with modeling, coupled with reflection, and is enhanced by ongoing dialogue.

Professional literature has explored the merits of job-embedded staff development for nearly a quarter of a century. In a 1977 report for the California State Department of Education, Joyce and Birdsall state that there "is very little job-related or job-embedded in-service education, and most of the important options for providing training are not being utilized" (p. 5). They surmise: "The enormous formal structure of school district and college related in-service appears to be much less effective than the help teachers give to one another" (p. 5).

ATTRIBUTES OF JOB-EMBEDDED STAFF DEVELOPMENT

Job-embedded staff development has three major attributes: relevance, feedback, and transfer. *Relevance* is guaranteed if learning is a part of daily work and addresses current challenges. *Feedback* is provided and encouraged from a variety of sources including peer coaches and administrators. *Transfer* of practice is integral; because the more transfer occurs, the more learning becomes embedded.

RELEVANCE

By definition, job-embedded staff development is job specific. It is designed to assist teachers in implementing best practices in their teaching. Training is not scheduled after hours at a remote setting. It takes place in the teacher's regular workplace, as a part of the normal work routine. Because job-embedded staff development becomes an integral part of the teacher's professional life, best practices can better reflect the individual context of the classroom to meet the needs of children while also addressing the learning needs of the teacher.

Teachers and administrators are no exception to the fact that adults tend to learn what is relevant to their professional and personal responsibilities (Wood et al., 1993). Because job-embedded staff development occurs as a part of the daily work activities of the participant, relevance is built into the experience (Wood & Killian, 1998). Relevance begins with "a thorough understanding of one's own ideology, personal philosophy, values, and beliefs" (Kraft, 1995, p. 35).

FEEDBACK

In *How to Organize a School-Based Staff Development Program*, Wood (1993) and his associates report that "in the absence of sustained support and attention, even successful efforts to change practice in schools will not endure (p. 44). This issue, one of the most neglected practices in staff development, is addressed by the second attribute of job-embedded staff development—continuous refinement using feedback from a variety of sources (Wood, 1989). Immediate feedback is provided through mentoring, peer coaching, self-reflection, and dialogue.

MENTORING

Wood and Killian (1998), indicate that a major advantage of mentoring is the ability of the mentor to help a colleague to identify weaknesses and suggest possible remedies. Two major benefits of mentoring are an increase in self-esteem through recognition and reduced feelings of isolation because of increased interaction with colleagues (Wollman-Bonilla, 1997).

PEER COACHING

Peer coaching was utilized to assist regular and special education teachers in their work in a study of children with Down's Syndrome (Kovic, 1996). The peer coach, Kovic, made use of a journal she kept during her in-class observations of the regular and special education teachers working together. Afterward, the three would meet to discuss what was observed so timely adjustments to practice could be made. The feedback offered by the coach was reported as continuous and objective; it encouraged reflection, problem solving, and immediate response to concerns.

REFLECTION AND DIALOGUE

Opportunities for meaningful dialogue can be created through the use of reflective questioning. Reflective questioning cultivates an atmosphere of learning where professional educators think aloud and "extend thinking through followup questions" (Lee & Barnett, 1994, p. 16). Reflective questioning is appropriate whenever a "personalized process of exploration is desired. It ceases to be truly reflective when the questions tend to lead the listener to a preconceived conclusion" (p. 17).

STUDY GROUPS

Study groups usually form around topics, by subject areas, by grade levels, or by special interest groups within the school. Groups promote ongoing dialogue and reflection. Key components of study groups include identifying a topic, area, or problem to explore. Once identified, the study group members need to develop a plan of action—who will do what—whether it be collecting schoolwide data or searching for information from the library. Functional study groups keep a journal of their discussions, findings, and plans of action. The group journal can prompt individual and collective reflection. Study group activities such as coaching and mentoring can promote acquiring new skills.

Team members who trust one another are empowered and are capable of providing more meaningful feedback (Calabrese & Zepeda, 1997). Study groups also provide a vehicle for collaboration with educators who possess a variety of skills and experiences (Murphy, 1992).

VIDEOTAPES

Storeygard and Fox (1995) found that videotapes were valuable in promoting self-reflection, as did Ponticell (1995).

The use of videotape is a natural extension of peer coaching. Teachers can pair up, videotape instruction, and then view the tape. Through questioning, the coach can help extend thinking. Videos of teaching can be maintained over time and viewed to discover what changes in practice have been made or need more refinement. Videotape analysis can be an invaluable tool in promoting reflection.

JOURNALS

Keeping a journal can also enhance reflection. This can be a journal kept by the teacher or by a colleague. Journaling allows the teacher to record events for reflection at a later time. Often, journals are used in conjunction with other staff development methods such as peer coaching (Kovic, 1996), mentoring (Wood & Killian, 1998), and study groups (Munger, 1995).

TRANSFER OF PRACTICE

One of the greatest challenges for staff developers is to find a way of ensuring the transfer of new skills into daily practice (Wood, 1989). Research demonstrates that only about 10 percent of teachers are able to transfer newly learned skills into daily practice (Hirsh & Ponder, 1991). A third attribute of job-embedded staff development is the immediate transfer of practice. Learning takes place on the job. Therefore, transfer of new skills into daily practice is also embedded in the process.

Teacher attitudes toward staff development can be a major obstacle to transfer of new skills into practice. A 1991 study asserts that "overall, teachers do agree that the purpose of staff development is to improve teaching performance" (McBride, Reed, & Dollar, 1994, p. 36). Unfortunately, the results of the study establish legitimate concerns for staff developers at every level. The study shows that 26.9 percent of teachers believe that staff development is based on legitimate needs; 25.2 percent agree that teachers actively use some information gleaned from attending workshops in their classrooms; and only 36.9 percent state that staff development provides new ideas or creative programs. Perhaps the most alarming statistic in the study is that only 12.6 percent of teachers surveyed report any meaningful followup to determine whether or not new skills were being used in the classroom (McBride, Reed, & Dollar, 1994).

ESSENTIAL CONDITIONS FOR SUCCESSFUL JOB-EMBEDDED STAFF DEVELOPMENT

Research demonstrates that certain conditions are essential for the successful implementation of job-embedded staff development. These include adult learning concepts, trust, time, and funding. Without any one of these conditions, efforts at effecting meaningful change are encumbered from the start.

ADULT LEARNING

Adults learn in very different ways from children. Because adults have multiple roles, tasks, and responsibilities, they bring a different orientation to learning (Smith, 1982, cited in Kraft, 1995). As a result, learning opportunities for adults need to be structured differently than those for children. Briefly, research on adult learning tells us that they need to perceive that the goals and objectives are both realistic and important to them as professionals. Learning opportunities need to be relevant.

Adults also need concrete situations where they can practice what they are in the process of learning. They desire feedback on their performance. In *The One Minute Manager*, Blanchard and Johnson (1982) stress the need for people to receive feedback in a direct and timely fashion.

Adults learn best in small groups and want to have a voice in what they learn (Wood et al., 1993). When these basic conditions are in place, learning for adults is more satisfying and most importantly, transfer of what is learned is more likely to become embedded in daily practice. For a more detailed discussion of adult learners, turn to Chapter 3.

TRUST

Change means leaving "what we are" and becoming "what we are not" (Barott & Raybould, 1998, p. 31). The unknown can be unnerving because we are leaving behind something with which we are comfortable. Fullan (1982) believes that "all real change involves loss, anxiety, and struggle" (p. 25). It is not surprising then that educators tend to resist change for a variety of reasons:

♦ The perception that change is a personal/professional attack;

♦ The history of change at the local/district site;

♦ The community/district reaction; and,

♦ The possibility of added individual responsibility and accountability.

Change also means admitting that there is a practice that needs to be modified. That is, we are admitting the existence of our humanity. For this reason, the issue of trust, the second necessary condition, is critical for job-embedded staff development to be meaningful. Teachers must be able to trust coaches, colleagues, and administrators, as well as themselves. Whether the development takes the form of mentoring, peer coaching, or reflection, teachers must be able to trust that feedback is constructive, is based on best practices, is grounded in research, and does not in any way constitute a personal attack.

Trust is essential for success in any form of coaching or mentoring. Costa and Garmston (1994) identify several areas in which a coach *must* build trust: in self, between individuals, and in the coaching process. Trust in self has been identified as a prerequisite for developing trust in any other area. A person must have a firm sense of his or her own values and beliefs before attempting to learn or implement new ones. Being consistent, open and accessible, nonjudgmental, and able to freely admit one's own mistakes are all characteristics of trust.

TRUST IN ONESELF

Teachers must, first of all, be able to trust themselves. They need to be able to develop a measure of objectivity when reflecting on their own practice. Artifacts such as journals, videotapes, and portfolios lose their effectiveness when teachers cannot be honest with themselves. Describing her experience as a peer coach, Kovic (1996) wrote: "I was no longer the expert, but…a co-learner and facilitator…I learned to trust my intuition, take some risks, make mistakes, and try again" (p. 31).

TRUST IN EACH OTHER

Secondly, trust must exist between individuals. This trust is established by knowing what is important to others, how they process information, and what their current thoughts and concerns are. Staff developers can demonstrate trust in others by spending time with them in unrelated activities, by inquiring about concerns important to them, and by displaying common courtesy (Costa & Garmston, 1994, p. 40).

TRUST IN THE PROCESS

Finally, each team member needs to believe that the process will be fair. This involves trusting the design of the process, the input of the other team members, and one's own input into the process. The success of any staff development endeavor is, in large measure, dependent on the effectiveness of its implementation.

Effective planning teams are successful in accomplishing the aims of an organization if they have the authority to recommend policies and procedures and to develop and implement action plans. Dysfunctional teams, on the other hand, are inherently destructive. This destruction can take the form of discord within the team or organization and results in a lack of focus (Calabrese & Zepeda, 1997). Team members can become embittered toward one another making any future staff development effort much more difficult.

GROUND RULES FOR PROMOTING TRUST

To facilitate trust among group members, certain ground rules are needed. These include:

- Creating a safe environment
- Selecting a facilitator
- Setting time limits for discussion
- Establishing the parameters of the group's authority

♦ Deciding what information will and will not be disseminated (Calabrese & Zepeda, 1997, pp. 188–189)

CREATING A SAFE ENVIRONMENT

According to Maslow, only survival is a more immediate human need than safety. The next level of Maslow's Heirarchy of Needs includes affiliation and social needs. In part, safety is "having things regular and predictable for oneself...and in-group" (Gage & Berliner, 1988, p. 337). Affiliation and social needs include "being recognized as a unique person with special abilities and valuable characteristics.... Others are aware of you and want you to be with them" (p. 337). If team members do not feel that they can share their ideas without fear of personal criticism, they will be wary of investing themselves in the team. While the merits and flaws of ideas should be critiqued, people should not be.

QUALITY FACILITATOR

A quality facilitator keeps all members involved equally in a project, making staff development efforts collaborative. Facilitating includes conducting the group decision-making process, building and managing agendas, maximizing the participation of all group members, resolving differences, and overseeing the planning of future steps (Costa & Liebmann, 1997). The main purpose of a facilitator is to make the work of the group as effective and efficient as possible.

TIME LIMITS

Limits for discussion are needed to ensure timely completion of tasks. In the heat of discussion, it is easy for team members to lose track of time (Calabrese & Zepeda, 1997). Tangential conversations can be detrimental to the efficiency of a team. These detours can cause the team to lose sight of the goal. Careful management of the clock increases the team's efficiency and helps prevent any one member from becoming too dominant a force on the team (Calabrese & Zepeda, 1997).

PARAMETER OF AUTHORITY

Knowing the parameters of a group's authority helps keep the members focused and helps prevent needless detours. The awareness of the extent of the team's authority can also prevent the potential embarrassment of making recommendations outside of the team's authority or unrelated to the team's desired outcome.

WHAT INFORMATION TO DISSEMINATE

Deciding what information to disseminate and when can prevent hurt feelings and dissension both in the team and among the faculty in general. Many ideas will be discussed and honestly critiqued. Some will be altered and others discarded. Although having one's idea discarded in favor of another should never constitute a personal attack, feelings of rejection naturally occur. Planning teams need to be sensitive to the feelings of their members.

TIME

As in any endeavor, learning takes time, which is the third condition for success. Creating time for staff development needs to be addressed from two perspectives.

RELEASING TEACHERS FOR LEARNING OPPORTUNITIES

Time is needed for reading, observation, collaboration, and reflection. Job-embedded staff development can help schools make the best use of their human resources by making the best use of time. Many schools shy away from implementing job-embedded learning because creating time during the regular school day for staff development activities is difficult. Traditionally, schools have scheduled 170–175 days of instruction and 5–10 in-service or professional days. These professional days are filled with teacher orientation meetings, parent-teacher conferences, teacher workshops, and other miscellaneous meetings. During regular school days, teacher schedules race at such a frantic a pace that continued staff development can easily fall through the cracks.

MOVING AT THE RIGHT SPEED

Like any other type of community, schools are complex. Implementing new practice occurs over an extended period of time (Bradley, Kallick, & Regan, 1991). Research shows that schools should be prepared to invest approximately four to seven years before seeing significant change take place within the organization. However, the time-intensive nature of change should not be perceived as license to move too slowly (Wood et al., 1993).

Accountability is an important factor in maintaining a realistic pace for school change. Staff development teams need to develop a time-line of benchmarks (Bradley et al., 1991; Calabrese & Zepeda, 1997). A time-line enables the team to observe progress toward full integration of a new practice into teaching. Benchmarks help sustain enthusiasm over the long haul.

FUNDING

Without adequate funding, which is the final condition necessary for success, job-embedded staff development is a severely disabled vehicle for school change. Release time for teachers becomes nothing more than a dream. The use of outside facilitators will be difficult to arrange. Human resources account for approximately 80 percent of most school districts' budgets. It behooves public education to make the most of such expenditures.

Given the lack of funds in public education, decisions need to be made on how funding for job-embedded staff development can be obtained. Two options are available to schools: find new funding or reallocate existing funding (Wood & Thompson, 1993). Funding should not be seen as a one-shot "inoculation" for the betterment of teaching practice. Procuring resources for staff development must be ongoing.

IMPLICATIONS FOR PRINCIPALS AS STAFF DEVELOPERS

What does a principal need to do to implement job-embedded staff development at the local school site? Based on the available research, principals need:

- To be *active participants* in job-embedded staff development initiatives.
- To empower and encourage teachers to take responsibility for their own learning.
- To participate in job-embedded opportunities for their own professional learning as principals.

Principals are key to any meaningful staff development program (Wood & Thompson, 1993). Therefore, principals must be *active participants* in job-embedded staff development. The message this sends to teachers is clear. If principals choose to value staff development and to actively participate, teachers will also choose to value staff development (Wood et al., 1993). Conversely, a lack of participation by the principal would be viewed by teachers as a "red flag" that indicates staff development initiatives are not important. Active principal involvement is, by its very nature, collaborative. This makes it possible for the principal to begin the critical process of team building.

Being an active participant in staff development does not imply that the principal must always be the leader. Sharing the responsibility for leading staff development efforts among faculty members is healthy in two ways. First, the principal is multiplying himself by involving others in the leadership of the school. The principal is able to spend time as a learner and as a collaborator.

A second benefit of shared leadership is the empowerment of teachers. It is the responsibility of principals to encourage teachers to take responsibility for their own learning. By placing a teacher in a position of leadership, the teacher is given the opportunity to practice skills seldom used in the classroom. Teachers become leaders not just in a particular staff development initiative, but also in the overall planning for the school.

Finally, principals need job-embedded opportunities for their own professional learning. Admittedly, it is difficult for principals to find time to do all the things already expected of them. It is also difficult for school districts, within the confines of limited resources, to create release time for principals. However, principals need time for professional reading, discussion of issues with their peers, and time for reflection (Orlich, 1989b).

A CASE STUDY FROM THE FIELD

Creating a Job-Embedded Staff Development Program
Evanston Township High School
Dr. Laura Cooper
Director of Curriculum and Instruction
1600 Dodge Avenue
Evanston, IL 60624
847-492-3808
e-mail: cooper@eths.k12.il.us
and
Renee DeWald
Chair, Staff Development Committee
and science teacher
e-mail: dewald@ethc.k12.il.us

CONTEXT

Evanston Township High School (ETHS) is a four-year comprehensive high school that occupies a 65-acre campus in Evanston, Illinois, a Chicago suburb. ETHS serves the city of Evanston and a small portion of the neighboring village of Skokie. Together the two communities offer an ethnic, economic, racial, and cultural diversity that is reflected in the student body. Nearly forty different language groups were represented in ETHS's bilingual education program in 1998.

The ETHS Staff Development Program involves all administrators, teachers, and teacher aides (about 250 participants) in groups that focus on topics directly related to improving student achievement, especially the achievement of students of color. The groups which are facilitated by ETHS faculty and staff meet throughout the course of a semester (seven to eight times) on special in-service and late start (for students) days. Because everyone is involved in a group, the program has had a significant impact on the professional culture by strengthening the norms of collegiality and experimentation.

PROCESS

In the spring of 1996, the Staff Development Committee submitted a proposal for redesigning staff development at ETHS. Functioning as a design committee of the School Improvement Team, the Staff Development Committee used its time to read and discuss articles on adult learning theory and on the research in professional development. This all-teacher committee decided that real school change would require an institutional commitment to adult as well as to student learning. The School Improvement Team's vision statement calls for the creation of a school in which "students, faculty, and staff must all continue to learn and grow."

The Staff Development Committee analyzed the existing professional development program and identified these concerns:

♦ Few programs provided for sustained learning experiences;

♦ Almost all programs were optional so many staff were not participating in any professional development, and

♦ Although the programs were beneficial to individual participants, there was no noticeable impact on the school's overall professional culture. The committee's proposal to the School Improvement Team recommended that all faculty have time and collegial support to participate in the school's improvement process. The administration and school board supported a restructuring of the school calendar and the addition of late start days.

THE "PILOT" PROGRAM

Faculty and staff were surveyed to identify critical instructional topics that are directly related to improving student achievement. From feedback, eight programs were established for the 1996-97 school year. Faculty with expertise in selected topics were recruited to serve as facilitators. The staff development groups met initially for a half day on one of the two opening of school institute days and on an in-service day in October. There were eight late start school days, four in fall and four in winter; on each late start day, staff met in these groups from 8:10 to 9:25 a.m. with classes beginning at 9:35 a.m. Despite the facilitators' nervousness over leading groups that included teachers who were skeptical about the value of teacher-led groups, the program was generally considered a success. The 1996-97 program evaluation showed that 76 percent of the faculty had experimented with new or remembered ideas related to improving student achievement. The results also showed that 85 percent believed that a sense of collegiality had been promoted in their group.

PROGRAM MODIFICATIONS

The first year of the program was successful, but several recommendations for improvement were made relating to program content, time, and group size. Some programs were added, some discontinued, and others were refocused. For example, the first year group on Improving Minority Student Achievement was too large (56 participants) and the scope of discussions too broad. Therefore, this topic yielded two smaller groups in 1997-98. One group continued to examine the research on minority student achievement by reading articles and bringing in outside experts. A second group identified ways that teacher expectations are influenced by ethnicity, culture, and gender. Participants in this group observed each other's practice. As program content was revised, an emphasis was placed on specifying the expectation that participants would make a connection between their learning and their work with students. The schedule was also modified to provide longer meeting times on the late start days.

PROGRAM EVALUATION

At the end of the 1997-98 sessions, the Staff Development Program Participant Survey was distributed, and 176 of 289 (61 percent) were returned. The results showed that:

- ◆ 72 percent of the responding participants had experimented with new ideas learned or old ideas remembered related to improving student achievement.

♦ 89 percent believed that a sense of collegiality had been promoted in their group.

The data on the experimentation question included 7 percent responding that they hadn't experimented and 21 percent giving other responses such as "not yet," "more time is needed," or "no response." Many of the 72 percent who reported experimenting with ideas did not just answer "yes," but added words such as "definitely" and "absolutely."

WHAT ARE THE CRITICAL RESOURCES?

ETHS's program to build staff development into the school day in a systematic way is dependent upon leadership from three groups: the school board, the administration, and the teachers and staff. The school board supported the proposal to change the traditional school calendar by creating a greater number of late start days for students in order to build a staff development program that would be connected with the board's top priority of improving student achievement, especially the achievement of minority students. The superintendent and other administrators demonstrated their strong support for the program by ensuring that all teachers were signed up and in attendance; administrators also actively participated in and, in a few instances, helped lead a group.

The staff development program, however, would not have been created or implemented without teacher leadership. A teacher-led committee proposed it and built support for it with other teachers, parents, and the School Improvement Team. Over the past 3 years about 50 different teachers and staff members have volunteered to cofacilitate a group. The administration has provided financial resources and training for the teacher facilitators.

FACTORS THAT CONTRIBUTED TO
THE PROGRAM'S SUCCESS

♦ Dedicated school day time when all faculty and staff are free to participate.

+ Small groups (no larger than 20 members) work best.

+ Recognition of outstanding teachers with expertise to share and good facilitation skills; having two facilitators in a group makes the tasks more manageable.

+ Summer time and grants for facilitators to reinforce their facilitation skills and to focus objectives for their group.

+ Strong administrative support with the superintendent expecting all administrators to participate and support the program.

+ A structural evaluation process that focuses on the goals of collegiality and experimentation with efforts to improve student achievement, especially for minority students.

+ Placing staff members, whenever possible, in their first choice for a group.

QUESTIONS

APPLICATION OF STAFF DEVELOPMENT PRINCIPLES

+ Statement: All staff development is job-embedded. Do you agree with this statement? Explain the stand you have taken.

+ What needs to be restructured in your school to provide for job-embedded learning?

ACTION RESEARCH

+ Identify a school or system that serves a culturally diverse population. Visit the site and look for markers that professional development is job-embedded. Report what you discovered.

+ At the same site, interview the principal to find out the types of resources that are needed to assist teachers in embedding their learning within the context of the school. Is job-embedded staff development cost efficient?

PUTTING STAFF DEVELOPMENT INTO A CONTEXT

♦ At your site, what would you need to do to ready the organization for moving toward job-embedded staff development?

SUGGESTED READINGS

Kovic, K. (1996). Peer coaching to facilitate inclusion: A job-embedded staff development model. *Journal of Staff Development*, *17* (1), 28–31.

Munger, L. (1995). Job-embedded staff development in Norwalk schools. *Journal of Staff Development*, *16* (3), 6–12.

Smith, C., & Beno, B. (1993). *Guide to staff development evaluation.* Sacramento, CA: Community College League of California. (ERIC Document Reproduction Services No. ED 363 381).

Wood, F. H., & Killian, J. (1998). Job-embedded learning makes the difference in school improvement. *Journal of Staff Development*, *19* (1), 52–54.

6

MODELS OF STAFF DEVELOPMENT

No stream rises higher than its source. Whatever man might build could never express or reflect more than who he was.

Frank Lloyd Wright

Before an architect's creation becomes a physical reality, it first takes shape as a blueprint. The purpose of the project is very carefully studied and needs identified. Next, a detailed plan unfolds. Diagrams that depict every facet of the completed project are produced. The architect knows what is to happen as each phase of the plan is completed. The desired physical outcome is predetermined. Success, however, is measured according to the needs the project was originally designed to fulfill.

Planning, conducting a needs assessment, and selecting a proper strategy are but a few of the necessary steps for ensuring success for a given staff development initiative. Unfortunately, no magical formula for designing and implementing appropriate staff development exists. For this reason, principals need to be familiar with existing models of staff development, identified through research, and practice, in order to determine how these models can be modified or combined to serve specific needs in schools.

Staff development, by its very nature, connotes and denotes change. Beliefs and values concerning teaching are challenged. Attitudes are reexamined. As a result, staff development has the capacity to redefine, reshape, and retool teaching practices. The redefining of practice entails decisions on the implementation of new strategies. Teachers should constantly be searching for new ways to help schools become learning communities, in general and in their own classrooms in particular. Reshaping practice involves melding new strategies with existing ones. Staff development does not necessarily require discarding existing strategies. It does require openness to new ones, however. Retooling requires that teachers utilize new strategies until they become fully integrated into practice. How this process takes place is as important as the fact that it *does* take place. This chapter presents different models of staff development and complementary processes that, when combined, can enhance adult learning.

Needs are as individual as the people and organizations that possess them. Staff development designs that work for one initiative might not work well for another. For this reason, a school with a polarized faculty might select general activities that promote team building and collaboration whereas a site implementing new curriculum standards might choose a plan that emphasizes specific teaching strategies.

Effective principals customize staff development by mixing and matching different models and methods. Therefore, staff development can be, and perhaps should be, purposely eclectic. For this reason, no particular model is championed in this chapter. It is for you to decide the merits of each model.

CHAPTER OBJECTIVES

- ◆ Identify various models of staff development.
- ◆ Describe processes that enhance staff development models.
- ◆ Identify implications for principals.

MODELS OF STAFF DEVELOPMENT: THE CLAY FROM WHICH INITIATIVES ARE FORMED

Sculptors mold clay into a seemingly endless variety of shapes. Each shape has a purpose and its own way of communicating a message. Each sculptor forms a bird or a human in much the same way. The uniqueness is found within the artist. Well-planned staff development initiatives designed by informed leaders (e.g., administrators, teachers, and staff) are analogous to the artist's clay in the hands of a master sculptor. In this chapter, various models of staff development are presented: RPTIM (Readiness, Planning, Training, Implementation, Maintenance), Individually Guided, Problem Based, Study Group/Cluster Approach, and Action Research. This list is, by no means, exhaustive; it is merely a starting point intended to assist the reader in the development of customized initiatives that will meet the individual needs of the school. Following the discussion of the models, complementary processes that can be embedded within those models are presented.

THE RPTIM MODEL

Based on research conducted in the late 1970s, the RPTIM model was designed principally by Fred H. Wood. RPTIM is a five-step readiness, planning, training, implementation, and maintenance approach that seeks to bring systemic change in schools. The RPTIM model is based on the belief that the local school site is the primary unit of change (Wood, Thompson, & Russell, 1981).

READINESS

Readiness is described by Wood, Killian, McQuarrie, and Thompson (1993) as essential. Readiness establishes favorable conditions for change. Four tasks need to be completed in the readiness stage. They involve building:

- A climate for and support of the desired change;
- Expectations for and commitment to change;
- Agreement on specific programs or practices to be implemented; and,
- Support from administrators, teachers, and the community.

Knowing how much time is needed to ready a staff is not easy. Wood and his colleagues believe that the readiness stage can last as long as three years. The higher the stakes, the longer the readiness stage lasts. Readiness needs can also reappear during the planning, training, implementation, and maintenance stages. It can be difficult to determine, in an exact manner, where teachers are as the group moves through the readiness stage. The more principals engage teachers in talking with one another, the more they emphasize the benefits of the proposed change, and the more they become informed consumers of the process and products of change, the better able they will be to meet these readiness needs.

PLANNING

The planning stage answers the question: "How will the goals formulated in the readiness stage be met?" First, define the specific objectives of the staff development initiative. Defining the specific objectives identifies what precisely teachers and administrators will be able to do as a result of their efforts. So that the planning team can know what teachers and administrators need to learn before implementing the new practice, a needs assessment is conducted. Next, identify available resources to support the initiative. The final task in the planning stage is to gain approval of the faculty and administration for the plan.

The principal's role in facilitating change is to remove obstacles to school improvement by:

♦ Providing release time for faculty;

♦ Arranging funding for initiatives;

♦ Involving everyone through activities that enhance collegiality, self-analysis, and reflection; and,

♦ Modeling active participation in staff development activities.

TRAINING

During training, there are four tasks to perform: select the appropriate in-service, recruit the trainers, develop a schedule of in-service, and provide necessary administrative support (Wood, 1989). During this stage, new information is disseminated to participants. Training can take place through such activities as in-service workshops, action research teams, full school groups, and learning clusters (Zepeda, Wood, & O'Hair, 1996).

IMPLEMENTATION

During the implementation stage, staff development moves from the controlled environment of in-service to the practical environment of the classroom. Principals need to provide assistance, give recognition, and supply needed resources to participants. The intended outcome of implementation is the transfer of new skills into practice. The failure of transfer, referred to as a "nonevent" by Wood (1993) and his associates, is the major pitfall during the implementation stage.

MAINTENANCE

The maintenance stage involves two major tasks: confirmation of the new practice and support for higher uses of the new practice (Wood, 1989). Maintenance can take many forms such as mentoring, peer coaching, self-analysis through reflection, reciprocal classroom observations, and collaborative dialogue among teachers and administrators.

THE INDIVIDUALLY GUIDED MODEL

It is possible for teachers to learn many things without the aid of a formal staff development program (Sparks & Loucks-Horsley, 1989). A design for the individually guided model was formalized in 1985 by Tracy and Schuttenberg. This self-directed model is designed to assist both the individual and the organization in achieving mutually agreed-upon improvement goals.

Self-directed learning utilizes many of the attributes of the RPTIM model, with the individual taking responsibility for the design, implementation, maintenance, and evaluation of their own learning (Caffarella, 1993). Because the teacher designs their own learning, its very nature is specific to the individual's needs. Its relevance is almost guaranteed.

Self-directed staff development can stand by itself, or it can be a part of the site or district's overall program. The individually guided model can work in concert with mentoring, peer coaching, and reflection, for example. This model also has the added benefit of convenience, since learning takes place when the learner is ready.

Purposes

Caffarella (1993) discusses the need for individual learning plans and the two purposes they serve. First, individual learning plans assist the learner in planning learning objectives for the coming year. This promotes individual selection of professional reading, participation in workshops, or involvement in any number of other staff development activities. The second purpose is to assist individuals in aligning their own learning program with school and district goals. Individual learning plans should be designed so that self-directed learning becomes an integral part of the teacher's overall individual professional development plan.

Role of the Principal

For the administrator who believes that teachers can facilitate their own learning, there is still a role for the principal. Although accountability is certainly a factor in the individually-guided model of staff development, an effective principal:

- ◆ Engages teachers in a process of setting learning goals;
- ◆ Provides assistance with the development of the plan;
- ◆ Secures resources for teachers (i.e., materials, travel funds, and release time);
- ◆ Meets periodically throughout the year to discuss progress and give feedback;
- ◆ Encourages creativity on the part of teachers;
- ◆ Connects teachers to others who are working on similar learning ventures; and,
- ◆ Helps teachers link one year's area of exploration to the next year.

THE PROBLEM-BASED LEARNING MODEL

GUIDELINES

The problem-based model of staff development utilizes real issues or problems to create an active, learner-oriented environment (Seifert & Simmons, 1997). Problem-based learning is rooted in participants' initial questions concerning the chosen issue or quandary (Gallagher, Stepien, & Rosenthal, 1992). Achilles and Hoover (1996) identify five guidelines for the problem-based model. An aim is for learners to be stimulated to build their own knowledge through the experience of some cognitive conflict or puzzlement (Savery & Duffy, 1995, cited in Torp & Sage, 1998). The process of the problem-based model includes:

♦ Identifying a problem situation with directions, guiding questions, and some resources for the learner to utilize;

♦ Letting adults develop clearly stated objectives;

♦ Minimizing boundaries so participants can develop their own format for solving the problem;

♦ Providing a realistic time frame for participants to solve the problem; and,

♦ Forming groups that elect their own leader or facilitator.

CHARACTERISTICS OF PROBLEM-BASED LEARNING

Engel (1991) describes problem-based learning as learning for capacity rather than learning for the sake of acquiring new knowledge (p. 21). Problem-based learning used as a model of staff development can provide opportunities for community members to choose their own area of study as it relates to practice whether it be in the classroom or in the larger context of the school. Problem-based staff development can be *learner-centered* or *problem-stimulated*.

PROBLEM-BASED LEARNING IS LEARNER-CENTERED

Problem-based learning that is learner-centered can be appealing to the adult who wants to investigate an area of practice that relates directly to his or her needs in the classroom setting. The learner-centered approach is not necessarily conducted in isolation. Often, several teachers identify a problem of practice and collaboratively explore the issues surrounding the problem. The principal supports the learner-centered approach by knowing the characteristics and needs of community members.

For example, if a principal hired five new teachers who had zero years of experience, the learner-centered approach would look different than a learner-centered activity for a group of teachers with five or more years of teaching. The principal is in a position to know that the issues of first-year teachers are different from those of experienced teachers.

PROBLEM-BASED LEARNING IS PROBLEM-STIMULATED

Problem-based learning that is problem-centered focuses members on a specific problem or a series of related problems within the community. The problem-stimulated approach can also be learner-centered as the issue under investigation can stem from a problem of practice by an individual who is facing a specific need, or by several people within the community who are experiencing similar issues.

The problem-stimulated approach can be a vehicle for the entire community to address a schoolwide issue. For example, if a high school is in the process of changing to the block schedule, the problem-centered approach could be used by the community to address the issues related to the organizational changes its people will face.

Both the learner-centered and problem-stimulated approach to problem-based learning can be used to assist teachers and the organization to grow, reduce isolation, and connect members of the community in a more focused and meaningful way.

THE STUDY GROUP/CLUSTER MODEL

Interest in study groups as staff development for professional educators began in the early 1980s. Joyce and Showers (1982) discovered that qualified trainers were no more effective at providing quality feedback to educators than were teachers themselves. This discovery laid the foundation for a long-term investigation using study groups to implement new practice into classrooms (Murphy, Murphy, Joyce, & Showers, 1988). The rest is history.

Study groups provide a conduit for teachers to become lifelong learners and, to a certain degree, to become action researchers. Because study groups provide an opportunity for teachers to focus on a topic that they choose for themselves, study groups help establish relevance for the individual. (For a more complete discussion of relevance, consult Chapter 5.) Study groups serve to promote peer interaction (Boggs, 1996) by providing more frequent opportunities for the sharing of ideas.

FACTORS FOR A SUCCESSFUL STUDY GROUP

The factors that contribute to the success of study groups are:

♦ Belief Systems

Study groups need a belief system that fosters the need for lifelong learning. Teachers need to understand that staff development is never a completed task.

♦ Administrative Support

Study groups need resources such as time and access to the latest research.

♦ Facilitator

The facilitator assists with developing and maintaining the group focus and manages each meeting. It is recommended that meetings:

• Last no more than one hour;

• Be held at the same time of the day;

- Be held in the same room and building; and,
- Foster the responsibility to try new ideas and practices. (Makibbin & Sprague, 1991)

Earlier models of staff development almost exclusively used an outside expert who would present and dash, rarely with any followup on what was presented. In this context, staff development, like change, was merely an event. Very little collegial interaction occurred; the facilitator did not know the audience, and the audience did not know the facilitator.

It is not being suggested that outside experts not be utilized. Outside facilitators serve a purpose if the conditions are set by the learning community prior to beginning the work. Suggested conditions for utilizing an outside facilitator include:

- Involving the facilitator in understanding the needs of the community;
- Utilizing the facilitator over a period of time to reduce anxiety for community members;
- Conducting ongoing evaluation of the impact of the facilitator in achieving staff development needs; and,
- Establishing a common language between the facilitator and the members of the learning community.

If the conditions are right, teachers and other members of the learning community can serve as facilitators. Utilizing teachers as facilitators of learning can serve as a stimulus for professional renewal.

NOTES FROM THE FIELD

Carlene Murphy is a professional staff development consultant and facilitator who has helped schools across the United States develop whole faculty study groups. The highlights of Murphy's Whole Faculty Study Group (WFSG) model are provided here with permission. Murphy's model is worth exploring as a means to help recast the roles that teachers play in charting their professional growth, enhancing the adult and student learning community, and in restructuring staff development to revitalize the organization.

Whole Faculty Study Groups

Carlene Murphy
961 Heard Ave.
Augusta, GA 30904
706-736-0756

Definition

Whole Faculty Study Groups (WFSG) is a structure through which all of the teachers on a faculty meet in small groups for serious conversation about student needs and classroom instruction. The small groups, called study groups, are comprised of individuals that join together to increase their capacity through new learnings to meet the needs of students. The study groups have an organizational focus, focusing on the goal of schools: student learning. It is a professional development process that allows individual teachers to design their own learning and to implement what they learn in their classrooms for the benefit of their students. The school's School Improvement Plan is the document that drives the process.

An Initial Assumption

For the process to begin, it is advised that:

♦ The whole faculty understands the WFSG process;

♦ The whole faculty participates in some form of decision-making process that acknowledges that a 75-percent majority to support WFSG will obligate all others; and,

♦ The whole faculty participates in reviewing student data that will guide all decisions about how study groups will be organized and what study groups will do.

The Functions of WFSG

WFSG's serve at least five functions. A study group may include all five as its purpose or only one, two, three, or four:

♦ To support the implementation of curricular and instructional innovations;

♦ To integrate and give coherence to the school's instructional strategies and programs;

♦ To target a schoolwide need;

♦ To study the research and latest developments on teaching and learning; or,

♦ To monitor the impact of innovations on students and on changes in the workplace.

Teacher collaboration is a byproduct of the WFSG process. To increase student learning is the primary purpose of WFSG and teacher collaboration is a means to that end.

Process Guidelines for WFSG

The following guidelines provide the structure the process needs to ensure the intended results.

♦ Keep the size of the study groups to no more than six;

♦ Don't worry about the composition of the study groups;

♦ Establish and keep a regular schedule, letting no more than two weeks pass between meetings;

♦ Establish group norms at the first meeting of the study group;

♦ Agree on a written Study Group Action Plan that is shared with the whole faculty by the end of the second meeting;

♦ Complete a Study Group Log after each study group meeting that is shared with the whole faculty;

♦ Encourage members to keep an Individual Reflection Log that is for their own personal and private reflection;

♦ Establish a pattern of rotating group leadership;

♦ Give all study group members equal status;

♦ Have a curriculum or instructional focus;

♦ Plan ahead for transitions;

♦ Make a comprehensive list of learning resources, both material and human;

♦ Include training in the study group's agenda; and,

♦ Evaluate the effectiveness of the study group, using the intended results stated in the Study Group Action Plan.

In summary, the question that guides all decision making in the WFSG process is: "What is happening differently in the classroom as a result of what teachers are learning and doing in study groups?"

THE ACTION RESEARCH MODEL

Kurt Lewin first popularized action research in the 1940s. Its first systematic application to education is detailed in *Action Research to Improve School Practice* (Corey, 1953). Action research acquired legitimacy in staff development in *Collaborative Action Research: A Developmental Approach* (Oja & Smulyan, 1989).

Marshak (1997) defines action research as:

A methodology through which teachers can formulate a research question that is central to their own professional practice, devise methods of collecting data pertinent to that question, enact data collection, analyze the data, articulate findings and conclusions that inform their teaching practice, and then change their teaching in ways indicated by the research findings and conclusions. (p. 9)

Action research is one type of applied research; its designs and methodologies are less rigorous so that individuals and groups are not encumbered with such tight controls as triangulation, discrete statistical applications, and auditing. Action research is, however, systematic in its approaches. (Glanz, 1998)

COMPONENTS OF ACTION RESEARCH

The steps that comprise action research include:

♦ Defining the focus;

♦ Developing research instruments;

♦ Collecting the data;

♦ Organizing and analyzing the data;

♦ Creating action plans; and,

♦ Reporting results. (Glanz, 1998; Marshak, 1997; McKay, 1992)

ACTION RESEARCH AS STAFF DEVELOPMENT

The design of action research staff development has several benefits:

♦ The opportunity to collaborate with one another;

♦ The development of a forum where interested members of the community can learn together;

♦ Learning opportunities that do not attempt to influence teachers toward a predetermined point of view;

♦ The opportunity to give emotional support to one another;

♦ Data-driven decision-making; and,

♦ More readily accepted change. (Watson & Stevenson, 1989).

Action research shows promise as a staff development model in that teachers and other members of the learning community are the researchers. As action researchers, teachers can study their practices, with data guiding informed discussions as well as the future decisions they make regarding their practices. Action research also promotes dialogue and reflection.

PROCESSES THAT ENHANCE MODELS OF STAFF DEVELOPMENT

Inherent in every model of staff development is the need for constructive feedback. Covey et al. (1994) refer to this process as feasting on the "lunch of champions," the "vision is the breakfast" and "self-correction the dinner" (p. 247). Through feedback, teachers can acquire the ability and humility to find the "blind spots" in their teaching practices (Covey et al., 1994). The following processes are explored: peer coaching, mentoring, reflection and self-analysis, and dialogue.

PEER COACHING

There are two basic peer-coaching configurations (Ackland, 1991). The first design involves coaching done by an outside specialist or expert (Brandt, 1982; Neubert & Bratton, 1987; Showers, 1985). The second design promotes reciprocal coaching by colleagues within the same department, teaching team, or campus (Christen & Murphy, 1987; Joyce & Showers, 1987).

According to Showers (1985), the design of a peer-coaching program includes:

- Investigating the climate for accepting change;
- Identifying specific issues to be addressed and observed;
- Training the faculty;
- Writing lesson plans that reflect new practices;
- Reviewing lesson plans in the pre-observation stage;
- Observing teacher performance; and,
- Extending dialogue during the post-observation conference.

FIGURE 6.1. A PEER-COACHING MODEL

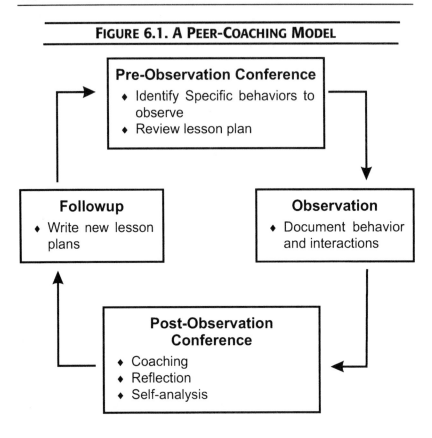

Pre-Observation Conference
- Identify Specific behaviors to observe
- Review lesson plan

Observation
- Document behavior and interactions

Post-Observation Conference
- Coaching
- Reflection
- Self-analysis

Followup
- Write new lesson plans

PEER COACHING AS SUPERVISION

Peer coaching affirms the sequential processes of the original clinical models of supervision (Pajak, 1993). As peer coaches, teachers need training and followup support to refine coaching skills. Coaches need training to gain skills in the areas of:

- Human relations and communication;

- Clinical supervisory processes: pre-observation, observation, and post-observation (feedback) techniques; and,

- The uses of data collection instruments (i.e., at-task, verbal flow, and classroom traffic).

MENTORING

All teachers, whether novice or veteran, have known many common emotions. Perhaps no emotion is as distressing as that of isolation. This feeling of isolation is enhanced by the compartmentalization of today's schools (Lortie, 1965). Teachers are placed into cubicles called classrooms, required to plan instruction for cubicles of time called class periods, and assigned to cubicles within the faculty called departments or teams. Mentoring is an effective tool for increasing collaboration among teachers.

DEFINITIONS OF MENTORING

Because of the complex nature of the mentor-protégé relationship, formulating a precise definition of mentor is a slippery proposition. Dodgson (1986) lamented that "the definition of a mentor is elusive and varies according to the view of the author" (cited by Carruthers, 1993, p. 10). Zey (1984) defines a mentor as "a person who oversees the career and development of another person, usually a junior, through teaching, counseling, providing psychological support, protecting, and at times promoting or sponsoring" (p.7).

Perhaps the most common use of mentoring in public education is for the induction of new teachers. Studies reveal that mentors fulfill numerous roles: provider of support and encouragement; confidant; conduit for information concerning school climate, culture, and policies; teacher; counselor; intervener; and sponsor (Ganser, 1996; Zey, 1984).

ATTRIBUTES OF SUCCESSFUL MENTORING PROGRAMS

Gehrke (1988) identifies eight attributes of mentoring:

- The mentor and protégé must have a voice in choosing each other;
- The administration makes release time available;
- The issues to be addressed are negotiated;
- The protégé demonstrates a growing independence from the mentor;
- The uniqueness of the relationship needs to be acknowledged;

♦ The relationship is reciprocal in nature;

♦ The participants feel free to discuss issues that go beyond the classroom; and,

♦ The participants must nurture dialogue. (pp. 44–45)

These are attributes of an ideal mentoring relationship; it is not expected that a mentoring relationship will exhibit all of these attributes all of the time.

REFLECTION AND DIALOGUE

Because of the natural cause and effect relationship between reflection and dialogue, they are considered together. John Dewey identifies three primary sources for knowledge: beliefs based on emotions, beliefs based on authority, and beliefs based on reflective thinking (Dewey, 1933).

Reflection is best understood as serious thought about a subject, as meditation, rumination, deliberation, and cogitation. Reflection serves as assessment, a vehicle for acquisition of skills, and as a conduit for self-directed learning. It provides direct evidence of teachers' attitudes and values (Caffarella, 1993). Reflection helps identify preexisting biases that can inhibit learning. Ongoing reflection also helps identify which issues are most pertinent to continue professional growth for the individual and, by extension, improvement for the school (Tracy & Schuttenberg, 1990).

RESEARCH ON REFLECTION

Research in the use of reflection has centered on how to prepare questions and how to ask the questions. Lee and Barnett (1994) identified four guidelines for preparing questions to be used in reflection. First, the respondent's experience should provide the basis for all questions. Because reflection implies the exploration of one's own experiences, questions not based on those experiences serve only as distractions. Second, questions should be worded in a neutral, nonjudgmental manner. Trust is an important condition for reflection. Therefore, questions should not contain language that implies evaluation, a sole correct answer, or that implies the questioner knows the correct answer. Third, the overall purpose should be served in some way with each question. The purpose should be agreed upon at the beginning of the conversation. Last, followup questions should be prepared in advance. The process of reflection breaks down if the questioner is not prepared for the next step.

In *Educating the Reflective Practitioner,* Schön (1987) provides an excellent analysis of reflective evaluation. He reports that reflection generates three levels of evaluation. First, new practice is evaluated in contrast to generally accepted practice. Is this new practice consistent with current research? Second, new practice is evaluated in light of past practice. How well can current practice accommodate this new practice? Last, new practice is evaluated in terms of the consequences of its implementation. What changes must the practitioner make in order to accommodate this new practice? What changes have occurred in the classroom as a result of using this new practice?

A CODA FOR PRINCIPALS

As the key to meaningful change at the school level, it is the responsibility of the principal to facilitate selection of initiatives that address the needs of the faculty, support training and implementation of new practice, and sustain maintenance of desired change. The purposes and needs for staff development initiatives are as varied as the people who implement them. Therefore, it is the obligation of the principal to:

♦ Maintain a current knowledge of research based staff development models;

♦ Share leadership for staff development; and,

♦ Be an agent of change in the school.

SUMMARY

The "purposely eclectic" nature of staff development was alluded to earlier because teachers' needs are eclectic. Therefore, to meet those needs, principals must be purposefully and demonstratively eclectic. Principals need to maintain current knowledge of models and processes of staff development in order to recognize when and how to use them as well as how to combine them.

No model stands alone and all models are containers of processes. Healthy schools employ a variety of models of staff development to meet the constantly changing variety of needs. The processes are job-embedded; necessary training for faculty to participate in them is not. For example, training can occur within a problem-based model or an action research model, but might not be recommended within a self-directed model. Staff development models coexist in empowered schools.

A CASE STUDY FROM THE FIELD

Paradigm Possibilities
Alan B. Shepard High School
Dr. Lois A. Stanciak
Associate Principal
13049 S. Ridgeland Ave.
Palos Heights, IL 60463
708-371-1111
stancial@sun.d218.k12.il.us

When I think of change at the secondary level, it reminds me of the story of Sisyphus in Greek mythology, forever condemned to push the stone to the top of the hill only to have to stand in the background to watch it roll helplessly down to the bottom again. Change is like that. Perseverance pays. In fact, it is one of the sure things in staff development that pays dividends in the long-term.

Over the past five years, a distinct effort was made to implement change at Shepard High School. To initiate and implement any change of substance, two things are needed: time and job-embedded staff development. The approach utilized at Shepard is the five Ps of the Paradigm Possibilities Process: *Planning, Preparing, Providing, Practicing,* and *Predicting.*

We had established an interest and belief in the importance of an integrated curriculum because of the benefits it generated for students and staff members. Although we have not reached our final destination, we are further along than we anticipated because of the five Ps.

PLANNING

Planning is the first step in the process. To be successful, we had to plan. There are specific skills and information that team members need before moving forward.

Certain areas were identified as essential to our immediate success. Because we were going to work in teams to integrate the curriculum for our students, we targeted:

- Change Process;
- Learning Styles;
- Thematic and Skill Driven Instruction; and,
- Consensus Building.

Next, we developed a time frame for learning about the specific topics, strategies, and skills needed for implementation. We began planning in January so that the workshops could be provided at the end of the school year and during the summer.

PROVIDING

Providing consistency for the workshops is an important consideration. Whether providing staff development for the program participants or the entire staff of 110, the format remains the same. Initially we began with 7 individuals; today, over 40 are involved in the program. The teachers are provided with:

- Time

    Teachers are provided staff development either during the summer, at early Saturday morning meetings, or during their professional period. Also, staff development is long-term.

- Ice breakers

    New and practical icebreakers are used that can be utilized with students in the classroom.

- Theory

    Teachers only need and want to know that whatever they are learning (e.g., Cooperative Learning or Learning Styles) has a strong, proven research base that improves student learning. They are more interested in the practical application in the classroom. Articles reporting research are made available to teachers, but limited time is spent discussing the content of these articles.

♦ Recursion

It is important to continuously build on previous knowledge.

PRACTICING

Paradigms will not be broken unless and until teachers have an opportunity to practice the new skill and/or strategy in the classroom. Feedback is needed and can be supplied in a variety of ways:

♦ New strategies can be practiced in Think, Pair, Share groups before leaving the workshop;

♦ Send teachers to workshops and/or training in teams to provide support and feedback for each other;

♦ Provide peer coaching, encouraging teacher teams to team teach and provide feedback to one another;

♦ Provide professional feedback from staff developers and consultants;

♦ Provide resources for teaching staff to utilize such as videotapes; and,

♦ Encourage teacher research to provide documentation for improved student progress.

PREDICTING

The last step in the process is not really a last step, but the building of a *Professional Community* where:

♦ Practices are expected to change;

♦ Learning and professional development are life-long, encouraged, and celebrated;

- Breaking paradigms is the rule, not the exception;
- Teachers document the change in student performance;
- Data is collected, reviewed, and used to make professional decisions; and,
- Collaboration, cooperation, and communication are the foundation for strengthening the school's climate.

We have continued to grow and to learn. As we checkoff our list of topics and strategies, we continue to add to the list as well.

QUESTIONS

APPLICATION OF STAFF DEVELOPMENT PRINCIPLES

- As the principal, you have been asked by the superintendent to explore cooperative learning with the three eighth grade teams. After reflecting on Stanciak's Paradigm Possibilities Model, outline what needs to be done at each stage. Keep in mind the context of the school and the characteristics of the eighth grade teachers and their students.

ACTION RESEARCH

- At your school site, examine a change that has occurred in the past year. What model of staff development would have better served the site? Analyze the effects of the change in relationship to any one of the models of staff development described in this chapter.

PUTTING STAFF DEVELOPMENT INTO A CONTEXT

- Conduct an audit of the teachers and staff in the building where you work. Examine the characteristics of the teachers who have been hired in the past two years and those of the teachers five years away from retirement. Develop a staff development plan for the newly hired teachers and those teachers who are five years away from retirement.

SUGGESTED READINGS

Glanz, J. (1998). *Action research: An educational leader's guide to school Improvement.* Norwood, MA: Christopher-Gordon Publishers.

Murphy, C. U., & Lick, D. W. (1998). *Whole-faculty study groups: A powerful way to change schools and enhance learning.* Thousands Oaks, CA: Corwin Press.

Wood, F. H., Killian, J., McQuarrie, F. O., & Thompson, S. R. (1993). *How to organize a school-based staff development program.* Alexandria, VA: Association for Supervision and Curriculum Development.

7

EVALUATING STAFF DEVELOPMENT: HOW ARE WE DOING?

Man is the measure of all things.
Protagoras
Fragment I

One of the key elements of any human endeavor is assessment. Doctors assess the physical or mental condition of their patients. Actors' performances are reviewed by critics. Figure skaters are evaluated by a panel of judges. Pencil and paper tests are administered to students across the country to evaluate how much they have learned. Education initiatives are evaluated to determine a measure of their effectiveness. Whether objective or subjective in nature, assessment is an attempt to measure value. The achievement of value is an important indicator of success.

In staff development, "value" is based on progress toward goals agreed upon during the planning of the initiative. The success of a staff development initiative is based on the extent to which *change* occurs. Goals can be written to initiate change within many different areas: student achievement, implementation of new teaching strategies, integration of technology into the classroom, or team building within the faculty. How does the principal know when transfer of a new practice has occurred? How does the principal decide whether or not student achievement has increased? Without systematic evaluation of efforts based on hard data, it is almost impossible to determine if lasting change has occurred.

CHAPTER OBJECTIVES

♦ Examine change as the object of educational evaluation.

♦ Identify the basic components of program evaluation.

♦ Identify implications for principals as evaluators of staff development.

CHANGE: THE OBJECT OF EVALUATION

The objective of evaluation in education is to measure change. Have teacher or administrator behaviors changed as a result of a given staff development initiative? Are these changes consistent with the original goals of the initiative? If not, why have they strayed from the original intent of the initiative? Answering these difficult questions is the central aim of educational evaluation.

What is change and what have we learned about change? Belasco (1990) believes that change is a process and not a product. The research of Hord et al. (1987) identifies six important characteristics of change. Their research concludes that change is:

♦ *A process:* meaningful change is a process which occurs over a period of several years, and is not a single event;

♦ *Accomplished by individuals:* change is not effected by groups of people or programs, but through the efforts of individuals;

♦ *A highly personal experience:* because each person is a unique individual, each person reacts to change in a unique way;

♦ *Incremental:* as individuals involved in change begin to trust and respect the new practice, they begin to grow in their ability to use it;

♦ *Understood best in terms of one's own practice:* a teacher tends to react to change in terms of what impact it will have on the teacher's classroom, students, planning, and time, for example; and,

♦ *Focused on the individuals involved in implementation:* first and foremost, change must focus on the people who will implement it, not on the materials to be used; materials do not effect change, people do. (pp. 5–7)

TYPES OF CHANGE

Schlechty (1997) identifies three different types of change: procedural change, technological change, and systemic change. *Procedural change* is an alteration in the order in which events occur, the pace at which they occur, or the configuration of events. An example is changing the sequence of procedures for enrolling a new student. These changes are usually of little consequence. *Technological change* occurs because of an advancement in technology. The use of computers instead of typewriters, for example. The job has not changed; only the tools used to complete the job have. *Systemic change* is a modification in the nature of the work being done. This involves changes in beliefs, values, rules, relationships, and orientation. Often, this type of change requires a metamorphosis of the very culture of the organization. Systemic change challenges the very roots of the organization. It should be no surprise that of the three types of change, systemic change is the least understood and the most difficult to achieve.

DIFFICULTIES INHERENT IN CHANGE

Change, because of its very nature, is a difficult concept for people in all walks of life. First, change means a *loss of control*. Nearly everyone wants some control over such aspects of life as health, happiness, and professional stability. If any of these are threatened, change is severely impeded.

A second reason why change is difficult is that it is *multidimensional*. One dimension of change is the use of new materials. Another dimension is the implementation of new strategies. Also, change involves acceptance of new beliefs (Fullan, 1982).

In teaching, change can be as minor as using a new brand of chalk or as major as adopting a new textbook with a radically different perspective from the former one. Technology is abundant with examples of new materials to be mastered: computers, graphic calculators, and the Internet.

For many teachers, the use of new approaches can be unnerving. Some teachers have fallen into the trap of using the same teaching strategies and questioning techniques day after day. The suggestion or mandate to implement new practice can be interpreted as an attack on one's competence as a teacher or, worse, on one's competence as a person. This apprehension can trigger a natural defense mechanism inherent in all people.

Perhaps the most personal dimension of change is the alteration of beliefs. At the very foundation of each person's psyche exists a paradigm as "...a model, theory, perception, assumption, or frame of reference. In the more general sense, it's the way we 'see' the world...a simple way to understand paradigms is to see them as maps..." (Covey, 1989, p. 23).

Frazier (1997) describes paradigms as "powerful expressions of how each of us perceives, understands and interprets our environments and our relationships with individuals and organizations" (p. 31). Challenges to our understanding tend to create fear which leads to resistance to change.

RESISTANCE TO CHANGE

Resistance leads to barriers to proposed change. Basom and Crandall (1991) identify these barriers to change in schools:

- *Interrupted sequence of leadership:* frequent changes in key leadership positions prohibit the creation of a climate for change;

- *Change is viewed as unmanageable:* too many educators do not believe that meaningful change is possible;

- *Poor preparation:* teachers and principals are frequently ill-prepared for the complex nature of change; conflict management and organizational behaviors represent new and forbidding territory to many;

♦ *Underrepresentation in the decision-making process:* teachers or administrators who are disenfranchised from the decision-making process have no ownership stake in change; therefore, they do not "buy in" to the process;

♦ *Tradition:* some teachers and administrators become so deeply attached to the way that they believe school ought to be that any change can be a very painful experience;

♦ *Competing needs and visions:* administrators and teaching faculty at times have difficulty agreeing on what changes are needed and how resources should be allocated; and,

♦ *Insufficient resources:* too many times, a lack of time and/or money derail the change process before it starts. (p. 74)

Once the barriers to change have been removed, beliefs and practices can be more readily open to change. These are the fruits of quality staff development initiatives.

DEFINITIONS AND COMPONENTS OF EVALUATION

What is evaluation? According to Smith and Tyler (1942), evaluation is "a process by which the values of an enterprise are ascertained" (p. 5). Gredler (1996) defines evaluation as "the systematic collection of information to assist in decision making" (p. 3). Evaluation is a process in which data is collected and analyzed for the purpose of rendering a qualitative or quantitative judgement on the quality of a given initiative.

PROGRAM EVALUATION OF STAFF DEVELOPMENT INITIATIVES

Staff development is but one of many types of programs found within the structure of public school systems. For staff development initiatives, program evaluation can provide information that "...systematically [determines] the quality of a school program and how the program can be improved" (Sanders, 1992, p. 3). Staff development needs ongoing evaluation to ensure that goals are being achieved, needs are being met, and that resources are being used wisely.

COMPONENTS OF PROGRAM EVALUATION IN EDUCATION

Like many human endeavors, there is no uniquely correct method for evaluating educational programs. Staff development is no different. However, there are some generally accepted evaluation processes that are particularly applicable to educational programs: selecting a focus, establishing an evaluation agreement, collecting data, organizing and analyzing the data, and reporting the results to stakeholders.

SELECTING A FOCUS

If an evaluation effort is to be beneficial to a school, precisely what is being evaluated needs to be defined. For any given staff development initiative, many aspects can be evaluated. Sanders (1992) identifies:

- *Program needs:* establishing program goals and objectives;
- *Individual needs:* providing for instructional needs of individual learners;
- *Processes or strategies used:* deciding what was effective, and why;
- *Outcomes of instruction:* determining, to what extent, students are achieving predetermined goals; and,
- *Site/district goals:* ascertaining whether or not site and/or district goals are being met. (p. 5)

Program evaluation can be both formative and summative. Formative evaluation is ongoing and can assist in identifying the need for revisions or midcourse corrections. For example, in the implementation of cooperative learning techniques in an algebra class, the teacher recognizes that some of the students have limited experience in working as a team. The midcourse correction could take the form of team building exercises for the class followed by reteaching fundamentals of cooperative learning. Summative evaluation is conducted at the end of an initiative for the purpose of assessing whether or not the goals have been met and what long-term changes need to be made. It is not uncommon for program evaluation to have both formative and summative components.

ESTABLISHING AN AGREEMENT FOR THE EVALUATION

Although not mandatory, it is sometimes helpful to have a written agreement that delineates the process (Ashur et al., 1991). The agreement should establish, in writing:

♦ *The focus(es) of the evaluation:* exactly what is and is not to be evaluated;

♦ *Who will be in charge:* who will have final authority over form and content of the evaluation;

♦ *How will the evaluation be conducted:* how and what types of data will be collected, when and by whom; also, how will the data be analyzed; and,

♦ *Who is responsible for distributing the results:* who is responsible for ensuring that all stakeholders are fully informed of the results of the evaluation.

With a written agreement, everyone involved feels a sense of ownership for the evaluation process. Written agreements also help reduce the fear often associated with program evaluation.

COLLECTING THE DATA

Data collection can take many forms. Some of these include questionnaires, observations, individual interviews, test scores, surveys, and followup training sessions (Keedy & Thompson, 1988). Test scores tend to be objective; the other sources tend to be subjective. Sanders (1992) provides guidelines for subjective data collection such as interviews and questionnaires:

+ Begin with easy, impersonal questions;
+ Avoid ambiguous questions;
+ Avoid leading questions; and,
+ Be aware of the respondent's knowledge level.

A second important consideration in data collection is deciding when the collection activities will occur. Sanders (1992), identifies three concerns in the timing of data collection:

+ *Due date:* use the due date of the evaluation to schedule backwards to when the collection should occur;
+ *Availability:* determine when the data will be available; and,
+ *Convenience:* collect data when it is convenient for participants; avoid rush times such as the beginning or end of the school year, exam periods, or holidays.

A final consideration when collecting data is deciding who will do the collecting. Will teachers and site-level administrators collect data? Are these people available at the time the data collection needs to be done? The principal might want to develop an evaluation team comprised of teachers and other interested parties. If this is the case, then release time, along with other types of support, will be needed. The principal might consider seeking assistance from faculty members from the local college or university.

ORGANIZING AND ANALYZING THE DATA

Wolf (1990) identifies three major steps in the analysis of data. First, data must be organized. Because a large number of variables are usually associated with an education study, data must be organized by variable. Because they are analyzed differently, quantitative variables need to be separated from those that are qualitative. The second step is the actual analysis of the variables. Last is the presentation of the data.

Organization of data is an important step in the process of identifying cause and effect relationships. Separation of data by variables allows the evaluators to view each variable's individual effects on the focus of the evaluation. For example, data from peer-coaching sessions needs to be analyzed separately from data collected during a followup training session for conclusions to be drawn concerning the effects of each treatment on a given practice. Qualitative data may also be organized according to subject or by question if a written instrument is used. This allows the evaluator to assess the effects of an initiative on different areas within a new practice.

REPORTING RESULTS TO STAKEHOLDERS

This is a crucial step in the evaluation process. How well results are communicated has a direct impact on the ability of decision-makers to respond properly. Smith and Beno (1993) suggest these components for the evaluation report:

♦ Goals that were established and why;

♦ Activities implemented to meet the goals;

♦ Persons who participated;

♦ Resources used;

♦ Satisfaction of participants;

♦ Impact on participants, specific programs and the institution; and,

♦ Recommendations for changes in the program.

Sanders (1992) divides the reporting process into three stages: identify the audience, choose an appropriate method for reporting, and followup to ensure evaluation is translated into a plan of action. Often, a formal report is given. Try to anticipate what questions your audience wants addressed. Members of the school board might have different concerns than the parent-teacher organization. Before finalizing the report, a draft should be circulated to key stakeholders for their comments.

GENERAL GUIDELINES FOR STAFF-DEVELOPMENT EVALUATION

Staff-development evaluation, like staff development itself, is a basic organizational process (Duke & Corno, 1981). Effective evaluation programs should have both long-term and short-term objectives (Rutherford, 1989). Short-term objectives usually target changes in teacher behaviors, in the school, or in the curriculum, while long-term objectives focus on improvements in student achievement or behavior. Staff development can be justified only if its ultimate goal is to improve education for students (Rutherford, 1989). Ellis (1986) reflects a philosophy that principals who are most successful in implementing improvements in practice, communicate their expectations clearly, provide appropriate technical assistance, and monitor results.

NOTES FROM THE FIELD

The cluster staff development initiative of Eisenhower Elementary School (Norman, Oklahoma) was highlighted in Chapter 6. Principal Pat Simons involved all cluster members in examining data collected and in framing how data results and recommendations would be reported to district-level administrators. Figure 7.1 illustrates the results of the first year's evaluation.

IMPLICATIONS FOR PRINCIPALS

Educational programs are inherently incomplete without a proper evaluation mechanism in place. It seems self-evident that the value and quality of an initiative remains a mystery if no one questions it. As staff developers, principals need to:

◆ Empower teachers to be evaluators of their own staff development; and,

◆ Be active evaluators of their own learning.

For principals to expect teachers to take responsibility for their learning, teachers need to:

◆ Have a sense of ownership for individual initiatives; and

◆ Feel "safe" to take risks in their learning.

Teachers need to be empowered to be evaluators of their own learning and, more specifically, of their staff development.

FIGURE 7.1. PROGRAM EVALUATION OF CLUSTER GROUPS

Plus	Minus	Think About
Talking with others—some concerns	Time away from teaching—overloaded it!	Sign up with individuals who are interested—possible provide subs if needed to continue
Valuable experience—good things came from it	Added to everything else	Cluster an extension of a committee
Time to set goals and implement them (positive experience)	Something else to worry about	Alternative activities
Have an opportunity to focus on something important to the individual person	Consultant only came once	What can we let go but continue to grow professionally?
Gain knowledge	Peer pressure to meet	Setting realistic goals
Professional growth	Different schedule	Integrating groups by more specific interests
Not being alone to gain information	Different needs and wants	Do we want to continue these next year?
New management ideas	Too big a task for small cluster	Ways to promote
Sharing ideas	Time	Create another vehicle to accomplish goals
Varied knowledge	Coordinating meetings	More negatives than positives
Colleague support	Diversity	Next year: Peer Mediation, New Math Series, Reading Sufficiency Act
Seeing progress	Absent members	
Sharing success	Other things on plate	

Teachers, who are disenfranchised from leadership roles in planning and designing staff development, will be reticent concerning its evaluation. Fear or perceived fear of retribution for honest evaluation of staff development initiatives will inhibit any meaningful teacher participation in that process.

As with any other phase of staff development, the most effective way for principals to show leadership in evaluation is through modeling. When teachers see principals evaluating their own learning, as well as participating in the evaluation of the school's learning, they are much more apt to be active in evaluation themselves.

SUMMARY

Nearly every human enterprise is evaluated in order to find an answer to the question, "Is it working?" In other words, is the outcome of the initiative worth the human and fiscal resources that have been invested? Change is a difficult, yet critical process. It is critical because properly selected and implemented change is the catalyst for individual and organizational growth. Principals are held accountable for the allocation of resources at the local site. Proper evaluation of all programs helps ensure proper use of all resources, and can assist the principal in making the case for further funding.

A CASE STUDY FROM THE FIELD

Collegial Support Teams
Ramirez Elementary School
Lucy Brown
Principal
702 Avenue T
Lubbock, TX 794014
806-766-1833

THE SCHOOL

Ramirez Elementary School serves a predominantly Hispanic and low-socioeconomic area of Lubbock, Texas. Approximately 95 percent of the 700 children who attend the school receive free or reduced-price lunches. The school campus is less than a mile from Texas Tech University. Since fall 1992, Ramirez has had a Professional Development School partnership with the Texas Tech University College of Education. Together the college and school have engaged in a number of collaborative programs to enhance the professional development of preservice and experienced teachers and faculty and the achievement and performance of both elementary and college students.

THE COLLEGIAL SUPPORT TEAMS INITIATIVE

For the past 3 years, the 42 teachers at Ramirez have worked with College of Education faculty members Dr. Judith Ponticell and Dr. Margaret Johnson to develop Collegial Support Teams (CSTs) as an alternative to the state's teacher appraisal system. The CST initiative began because both teachers and administrators were looking for ways to improve teaching and learning. Both believed that the state-required appraisal system (essentially a once-a-year observation by an administrator using an appraisal instrument based on a direct-instruction model) had done little to enhance teachers' professional improvement. Dr. Ponticell helped us determine what supervisory and professional development approaches might provide Ramirez teachers and administrators with the outcomes we were looking for. She then provided training and support as the CST concept was developed, implemented, and refined. Dr. Johnson assisted us as we studied the effects of our CSTs on collegiality, experimentation, and instructional change.

CST OBJECTIVES

The Collegial Support Team has three purposes:

+ To increase professional collegiality;
+ To develop a school culture that supports critical examination of instruction and experimentation; and,
+ To develop a sense of collective responsibility for professional improvement and student achievement.

CST PROCESS

All teachers participate in a Collegial Support Team. The teams were constructed by the principal in collaboration with the teachers. CSTs hold regular meetings, engage in peer supervision cycles, and determine professional development opportunities. In addition, teachers with three or more years experience can use their CST work as their only form of teacher evaluation. Teachers with one to two years experience participate in a CST but are also evaluated by the principal using the state-required system.

A CST involves seven teachers across grade levels—kindergarten through sixth grade. Children move through the grades in cohort groups with the teachers in a particular CST, thus forming five small "schools" within the school. Subject specialist teachers are grouped in separate teams. CSTs provide a vehicle for continuous professional development. A CST meets every week to discuss professional concerns. Some of these may include practical matters such as scheduling visits or conferences; others may include team/school initiatives such as curriculum alignment. Still others include collaborative professional dialogue about teaching and learning concerns. Within each team, teachers choose partners as peer supervisors. Peer supervision partners engage in coaching cycles that include a previsit conference, a classroom visit, and a post-visit conference. While teachers work primarily with their peer supervisors, they also visit other teachers' classrooms to develop networks of professional resources.

At the beginning of the year, teachers prepare a professional development contract explaining their professional goals for the year. The contract is discussed with the CST and principal, and it is signed by all members. During the year teachers prepare professional portfolios. The portfolio provides evidence of a teacher's progress toward the goals set at the beginning of the year. Portfolios are a frequent focus of the professional dialogues among CST members. Teachers also videotape their classrooms and conferences with their CST peer supervisors. Selected video clips are included in the portfolios. At the end of the year, teachers evaluate the progress they made toward their professional goals for the year.

They also write a reflective essay describing their professional improvement. The evaluation of their professional development, their essay, and their portfolio are discussed with CST members and are finally presented to the principal.

EFFECTS OF THE CSTs

Have the CSTs had the effects that we had hoped for? Both action research and program evaluation over the three years that the CSTs have been in place indicate yes:

- ◆ CSTs have increased teachers' willingness to address instructional and curricular weaknesses.
- ◆ CSTs have increased teachers' participation in professional development opportunities, including graduate courses.
- ◆ CSTs have led to greater experimentation with new instructional and curricular approaches. Most importantly, experimentation was based upon information and sound rationales addressing students' needs and performance goals.
- ◆ CSTs created smaller, more personal units of teachers and students and enhanced vertical planning.
- ◆ CSTs developed a collaborative culture where teachers felt a responsibility for each other's professional improvement and held each other accountable for that improvement.

SUPPORT OF THE CSTs

The Professional Development School partnership with the College of Education at Texas Tech enabled training, ongoing problem-solving research, and program evaluation support from university faculty. Monies for private consultants for additional professional development opportunities were available through school and district staff development funds.

A teacher's workload increases with a CST. The processes involved take time. Teachers determine when meetings and peer supervision cycles take place. CSTs generally meet weekly after school; professional dialogues occur, portfolios are assembled and discussed, pre- and post-visit conferences occur during those times. Time for classroom observations is facilitated by the principal who works with teachers to determine schedules and secure substitute teachers.

The principal's role in instructional improvement changes. The principal applies for and secures district or state waivers needed to initiate an alternative teacher appraisal system. He or she also arranges time for training and funds to support staff development. The principal also becomes a participant in training, so that the principal understands the rationale and goals of the teachers' work so as to better facilitate that work. The principal's primary work as a supervisor and evaluator becomes the development of the teacher's capacity to engage in these processes.

IN SUMMARY

Any number of educators have urged teachers to open their classroom doors—and themselves—to professional improvement. The Collegial Support Teams at Ramirez Elementary School did this. It is important to note that the CSTs are entering their fourth year. It has taken us three years to develop and refine our processes, receive training, gain confidence, garner support at the district and state levels, and realize benefits. We took the time, aggressively sought the support, and studied the effects of our efforts. What we have learned suggests that Collegial Support Teams, given such time and support, foster both personal and institutional professional growth.

QUESTIONS

APPLICATION OF STAFF DEVELOPMENT PRINCIPLES

- ◆ Why do staff development activities and initiatives need to be evaluated? What types of evaluation are most important?
- ◆ Examine a staff development initiative that is currently in place at the school in which you work.

What types of data are being collected? What is being done with this data?

ACTION RESEARCH

♦ Work with a building-level administrator to design an ongoing evaluation of a staff development program already in place. Present the evaluation design to the class.

♦ In your setting, examine how staff development is evaluated. What data indicates that staff development has had an impact on:

- Student achievement
- Implementation of process and content standards
- Teacher development?

Prepare a presentation for the PTA or school board that addresses these program evaluation results.

PUTTING STAFF DEVELOPMENT INTO A CONTEXT

♦ Why are most teachers fearful of evaluating staff development initiatives? What typically is done with the information from evaluations?

SUGGESTED READINGS

Frazier, A. (1997). *A roadmap for quality transformation in education*. Boca Raton, FL: St. Lucie Press.

Gredler, M. (1996). *Program evaluation*. Englewood Cliffs, NJ: Prentice-Hall.

Schlechty, P. (1997). *Inventing better schools*. San Francisco, CA: Jossey-Bass Publishers.

8

Funding Initiatives: The Principal as Entrepreneur

Nature makes merit, and fortune puts it to work.
Francois de La Rochefoucauld

One of the greatest challenges of the principalship is the management of limited resources to meet seemingly unlimited needs. This task is further complicated by competing programs championed by stakeholders including teachers, students, parents, community leaders, and central office administrators. McCall (1997) states that *"the budget is key because it encompasses the financial crystallization of an organization's intentions"* (p. 69, emphasis in the original).

Public schools across the United States invest considerable sums of money in their teaching faculties. Annually, this investment totals more than $157 billion. Expenditures for teaching salaries, benefits, and instructional supplies comprise 62 percent of local school budgets (U.S. Department of Education, 1998). Including noninstructional personnel such as guidance counselors, nurses, therapists, business personnel, and administrators, personnel expenditures for public school districts account for approximately 80 percent of local budgets (Thompson & Wood, 1998).

An ongoing, properly designed staff development program is essential if schools are to reap maximum benefit from the investment in teaching faculties. Most district staff development programs are line items; however, it is even more important that funds are allocated to individual school sites.

Unfortunately, resources from within the budget are rarely sufficient for all staff development needs. Therefore, principals need to become entrepreneurs to meet site needs.

CHAPTER OBJECTIVES

- ♦ Identify alternative strategies for funding staff development initiatives.
- ♦ Explore the role of the principal as entrepreneur.

STRATEGIES FOR FUNDING STAFF DEVELOPMENT

BUILDING THE BUDGET

A school district's priorities are reflected in its budget. Guthrie, Garms, and Pierce (1988) describe the relationship between budget and program as follows:

> It is through budgeting that an organization aligns its resources with its purposes. Also, the budget process is the concrete, practical link between *planning*, the forward-looking portion of an organization's management activities, and *evaluation*, which focuses systematically on past performance. (p. 223, emphasis in the original)

At the beginning of every school year, principals are faced with the same dilemma: how to adequately fund every need within a finite budget. Thompson and Wood (1998) identify four steps in the budgeting process:

- ♦ Estimate available revenue;
- ♦ Envision the educational program;
- ♦ Determine the required expenditures for the program; and,
- ♦ Make decisions to balance program needs against available revenue. (p. 119)

ESTIMATING AVAILABLE REVENUE

Principals receive their budgets from the central office. It is from these funds that most staff development initiatives are funded.

ENVISIONING THE EDUCATIONAL PROGRAM

Envisioning programs is the process of determining which existing programs to maintain, which are in need of improvement, and what new programs need resources (Thompson & Wood, 1998). This process is an extension of the program evaluation process. The envisioning process can become a powerful tool for stakeholder empowerment (McCall, 1997). If a program is determined to only require maintenance, then prior years' budgeting information might be sufficient for setting the current year's budget.

DETERMINING THE EXPENDITURE REQUIRED TO SUPPORT THE PROGRAM

At this stage of the budgeting process, numbers are assigned to each line item in the budget. Personnel costs are determined based on state mandated formulas and projected enrollments. Other costs such as professional development, transportation, and food service are evaluated at this time (Thompson & Wood, 1998).

BALANCING THE BUDGET

The final stage of budgeting is the comparison of revenue availability as determined in the first stage with the cost analysis completed in the third stage (Thompson & Wood, 1998). The bottom line is now addressed. Is there enough revenue to cover projected costs? The nature of school revenue dictates that some needs may not be manageable. Perpetually growing needs in public schools will require the twenty-first century principal to be a fund-raising manager.

STRATEGIES FOR FUNDING STAFF DEVELOPMENT

This chapter discusses three alternative strategies for funding staff development: grant writing, foundations, and business partnerships. This list should in no way be considered exhaustive. It is intended to provide a starting place for principals needing additional funding for staff development initiatives.

GRANTS AND GRANT WRITING

Grants are awarded to organizations to address specific concerns. Funding from grants may assist schools in hiring additional faculty, purchasing supplies or needed equipment, or covering the cost of traveling to workshops (Norton & Kelly, 1997). Van Ness and Van Ness (1978) identified five steps in acquiring grant funding:

♦ Assessing needs and setting priorities;

♦ Identifying prospective donors;

♦ Educating and cultivating prospects;

♦ Submitting the proposal; and,

♦ Exhibiting good stewardship. (pp. 4–6)

Institutions tend to have specific interests that they wish to fund. These funding agencies want to know what problem needs to be addressed, specifically how needs will be met, and precisely what will be purchased with funds should the agency make them available (Ruskin & Achilles, 1995). Successful grant proposals address needs that are consistent with the interests of the funding organization.

Geography can also be an important consideration when developing a prospective donor list. Some institutions only fund proposals from specific areas. These can be narrowly defined as certain cities or as broadly as a specific state or group of states. Helpful resources for finding private institutions which have grant programs can be found in foundation directories published in most states (Van Ness & Van Ness, 1978). Past giving is another important tool for developing a prospective donor list. Many institutions publish an annual report which lists grants bestowed, to whom, in what amount, and sometimes for what purposes.

Educating prospective donors concerning needs is an important step. If an officer or board member of the funding institution is known to the local school system, personal contact is a way of making your proposal stand out from the rest.

When no contact is present, educating the prospective donor must be done through the proposal. Personal delivery of a proposal increases the odds of success (Van Ness & Van Ness, 1978).

Newcomb (1996) identifies eight principles for writing successful proposals:

- ◆ Contact the funding agency first. Ask for pertinent writers guides, forms, and any other information that is available about their grant giving.

- ◆ Prepare a preliminary proposal or a summary of your project.

- ◆ Have several colleagues or interested individuals read and comment on your ideas. Look for groups or individuals to endorse your project. These are helpful additions to your final grant proposal, and many times, are required by the grant giving agency.

- ◆ Do your homework. Research and become an expert on your topic of interest. Try to find out who will be competing with you for grant monies.

- ◆ Write your grant using all the research, information, and guidelines you have put together. Use the forms you have obtained from the agency.

- ◆ Be neat, be professional, and be accurate in your proposal. Show that you are confident with your ideas and your abilities.

- ◆ Have a neutral person proof, check, and review your final project draft. Be ready to answer questions or accept suggestions for improvement or clarity.

- ◆ A cover letter of transmittal should always be used when sending in your grant request. (p. 7)

It is also important to remember that officers of grant-giving institutions read many proposals. Time constraints necessitate brevity. An important responsibility of any grant recipient is to be a good steward of monies entrusted to the recipient's organization. Few attributes will destroy the ability of an organization to secure future funding as wasting existing resources (Van Ness & Van Ness, 1978).

FOUNDATIONS

Federal and state foundations often sponsor programs in public schools. An excellent source of information on foundations is the *National Directory of Corporate Giving* published by The Foundation Center of New York (Norton & Kelly, 1997, p. 16). Because the process of obtaining funding from national foundations is extremely competitive, public schools have employed alternate strategies to increase the probability of success. One such strategy is submitting joint proposals with school systems who have similar or complementary needs. Another recently developed strategy for acquiring funding is the establishment of local education foundations (LEFs).

LOCAL EDUCATION FOUNDATIONS

A new phenomenon in school funding has recently emerged—the local education foundation. As defined by de Luna (1995), "local public education foundations are nonprofit, income-tax-exempt entities that usually operate independently of the school district to promote educational excellence and innovation" (p. 1). Local education foundations are developed primarily in response to decreasing tax revenue resulting from changes in tax laws. Currently, there are more than 2,000 local education foundations nationally (Henry, 1995).

Local education foundations are usually founded by parents and local business leaders in cooperation with school leaders. A planning committee is formed (for purposes of incorporation an attorney is needed) and usually serves as the first board. The governance is separate from that of the local school district.

Money is raised in several ways by local foundations: dinner theaters, formal banquets, golf tournaments, fashion shows, auctions, and raffles. A local education foundation's spending is determined by its board. Expenditures include curriculum innovations, teacher training, and scholarships.

A few LEFs raise enough money to fund additional teaching positions (Merz & Frankel, 1995; cited in de Luna, 1995).

BUSINESS PARTNERSHIPS

A third strategy for raising additional revenue for public schools is creating partnerships between schools and local businesses. By matching school needs with local business interests, prospective donors with an interest in helping may be located. Resources from business partnerships may take a variety of forms. The most common are cash, supplies, and personnel (Norton & Kelly, 1997).

Ruskin and Achilles (1995) identify five steps to establishing mutually beneficial partnerships with businesses:

- Identify the needs to satisfy through partnerships;
- Select the businesses to be approached;
- Determine strategy for approaching the businesses;
- Prepare for the visit; and,
- Send a personalized thank you note. (pp. 37–38)

IDENTIFY NEEDS

Data collected from a variety of sources is most useful for identification of needs. This is especially true of staff development. Possible information sources include direct classroom observation, artifacts such as discipline referrals, lesson plans, curriculum guides, and faculty interviews (Wood, 1989).

SELECT PROSPECTS

Perhaps the most important principle in selecting prospective donors is to match school needs with business interests because businesses tend to assist in meeting those needs in which they have a *vested interest*. For example, a business in need of workers with strong mathematical backgrounds might be interested in underwriting the cost of integrating the use of technology in mathematics classes and the professional development necessary for the mathematics faculty to implement targeted changes. The state department of commerce or state department of education can be helpful at this stage (Ruskin & Achilles, 1995).

DETERMINE STRATEGY

There are three main methods of approaching a business during a fund-raising campaign: in writing, by telephone, or in person. Letters and telephone calls are most useful when time is at a premium. A large number of potential contributors can be contacted in a relatively short period of time. The investment of personnel in the fund-raising process is minimal. Unfortunately, letters and telephone calls are the least effective methods of fund-raising. Letters are too easily misplaced or, worse, ignored. Telephone calls may go answered. It should be understood that secretaries and receptionists increase their bosses' efficiency by minimizing interruptions. Decision makers can be difficult to reach by telephone.

Personal contact is the most effective way to raise funds. First, a request made in person is much more difficult to decline than a letter or telephone call. Body language, an important part of interpersonal communication, is a factor only in personal contacts. Second, by setting an appointment and making the request in person, communication directly to the proper person is assured.

Perhaps the most important component in personal contact fund-raising is having the *right people do the asking*. Small groups, usually three or less are best. A large group can have the appearance of an ambush, which could make the potential donor feel uncomfortable. There are two key people in the visiting group: the "explainer" and the "asker" The explainer is a representative of the school whose purpose is to answer any questions the potential donor might have about the innovation. The explainer should have a one-page description of the initiative prepared for the donor. Other materials pertaining to the innovation should be available in case further explanation is requested or needed.

The real secret to success in the fund-raising process is identifying and recruiting the best asker. This person should be someone whom the potential donor knows and trusts. It might be a person with whom the donor plays golf, dines out, or attends club meetings. Because the asker knows the donor, the asker knows *how* to ask. The asker will know the approach that is most likely to elicit a favorable response.

PREPARE FOR THE VISIT

Preparation for the visit is very important. In any setting, whether rural, suburban, or urban, a brief, well-prepared presentation demonstrates respect for the potential donor's time. Determine ahead of time what each person will say and when. The asker usually does most of the talking. Also, make sure the donor has ample opportunity to contribute to the conversation. After all, this is the beginning of a partnership.

Do your homework concerning the potential donor. Be aware of the number of employees and the type of work they do (Ruskin & Achilles, 1995). Much of this information is usually collected prior to donor selection. Before this first meeting is concluded, firm followup plans are agreed upon. Without the next steps clearly delineated, the budding partnership may fizzle.

FOLLOWUP

It is imperative that donors know that they are appreciated. For this reason, a personalized thank-you note should be written *the same day as the meeting*. A tardy thank you has almost the same effect as not sending a note. Nurturing is necessary for the partnership to continue to grow—this is the first step. Be sure to emphasize how important this donor is to the school (Ruskin & Achilles, 1995).

THE PRINCIPAL AS ENTREPRENEUR

Principals on the threshold of the twenty-first century have to be more than mere managers. Perpetually tight budgets, coupled with added social expectations, continually challenge the creativity of school leaders. Principals need to be entrepreneurs.

The Center for Entrepreneurial Leadership (cited in Miner, 1997) defines entrepreneurs as "independent profit-seekers who are working to innovatively exploit an identified business opportunity" (p. 103). Gerstner et al. (1994) describe an entrepreneur as "the person who reconfigures uses of capital and labor. The entrepreneur may be a risk-taker; indeed, frequently is a risk-taker...but...does not take risks for their own sake" (pp. 33–34). Gerstner and associates also state: "Typically, the biggest 'risk' the entrepreneur takes is to swim against the tide of the conventional wisdom" (p. 34).

Successful principals are educational entrepreneurs. They create innovative, ongoing opportunities for staff development to occur. This new breed of principal has the confidence to identify the right opportunities to take risks. Principals who are entrepreneurs empower teachers to create new ways of structuring time, raising funds, and being leaders. They are also capable of originating prototypical and cost effective ways of creating release time for teachers to participate in staff development activities.

SUMMARY

This chapter shed light on a new role principals need to master—that of educational entrepreneur. Principals of twenty-first-century schools must be innovative risk takers to continue meeting growing needs with limited resources. Alternate sources of funding and methods of harvesting that funding need to be found. Time must be restructured as a valuable resource to be used wisely, and not allowed to become an artificial prison.

A CASE STUDY FROM THE FIELD

Buying Time for Professional Development
Martha Burger, Ed.D.
Principal
Plato Elementary School
PO Box 1548
Duncan, OK 73534
580-255-6167
plato@texhoma.net

CONTEXT

Plato Elementary School (Duncan, Oklahoma) is located in rural southwest Oklahoma. Plato enrolls approximately 325 students in grades K-6. Test scores generally range between the 70th and 80th percentile. There are a growing num-

ber of students from single-parent families and with de-
prived backgrounds. As a result, teachers are having to
rethink whether the way they teach is meeting the needs of all
students.

Because we are in a rural area, somewhat isolated from
larger cities and major universities, one of our difficulties is in
helping teachers to stay current with educational thought
and trends. As principal, part of my responsibility is to provide and facilitate staff development for teachers so they can
enhance their instructional practices.

PROCESS

"Buying Time for Professional Development" is the term I
apply to an ongoing effort to provide building-level staff development. We need a way to build a common vocabulary
and develop a set of beliefs that we can support. My central
goal is to transform my staff into a team working toward a
common goal.

To create this learning community, I initiated several different types of programs, including a special workday, which
I call a "faculty retreat," before teachers report for duty at the
beginning of the year; whole-faculty planning time, which is
made possible by volunteers who teach classes while teachers meet together; and scheduling classes so that grade-level
teams have a one hour block of time together each week for
planning. Buying or stealing staff-development time whenever and wherever I can find it, provides learning opportunities for teachers and staff.

The faculty reaps several benefits from this special time.
First, it is informal. Teachers freely participate as a team without the usual distractions. With the help of some staff members, we are able to address specific needs of our school. This
is the time when we can explore our belief systems and reflect
on our mission statement. We can talk about the kinds of students we are dealing with and the needs they have, and we
can come to consensus on how we as a faculty will address
these issues. Once school starts, we are generally so deep in
the forest that we can't see the trees.

Opportunities were created during the regular school day
for the faculty to spend time (usually two or three hours) to-

gether. We created a program called eXL, short for eXtended Learning Activities. With the help of teachers and parents, we found people to come to our school to teach special arts activities to the students while teachers met to plan themes and related activities for the following year. The volunteers taught the same class twice, 50 minutes each time. Students could then select and attend two of the classes. A program that made it possible for teachers to work as a whole-faculty study group also gave students some very special learning opportunities.

At first, our faculty did not understand why they needed block planning time. Several didn't know how or why to plan collaboratively. I wanted them to use the time to discuss goals for the year, to plan special activities in advance, to develop our theme for the year, to explore ways of being more effective, and to help each other solve student discipline and learning problems.

In addition to buying or stealing staff development time, I try to put as many informational items as possible in writing, so that our time might be used more profitably.

SUMMARY

To me, staff development has as much to do with molding a staff to fit the needs of the school as it does with offering teachers workshops at which they can enhance their own skills. My responsibility is to be the person who upsets the equilibrium, questions the status quo, and encourages the faculty to stretch their thinking about student needs.

QUESTIONS

APPLICATION OF STAFF DEVELOPMENT PRINCIPLES

♦ After reading Dr. Burger's Case Study, develop a plan for professional development activities that is realistic to the situation at your site.

ACTION RESEARCH

♦ Interview a K-12 principal about the relationship between the site level and the district level in finding resources for staff development. What insights did you gain from this discussion?

♦ Visit a school that has a partnership with a local business that assists with resources to provide professional development. Provide a program description that includes:

- Goals and objectives
- An accounting of what steps were taken to establish the partnership
- The benefits to students and teachers
- The pitfalls to avoid

PUTTING STAFF DEVELOPMENT INTO A CONTEXT

♦ If you were to attempt to experiment with the format of staff development at your site like Dr. Burger did, what types of opposition and support would you expect from the district? Teachers? What would you do to coordinate individual site-level initiatives with those of the district?

SUGGESTED READINGS

Gerstner, L., Semerad, R., Doyle, D., & Johnston, W. (1994). *Reinventing education: Entrepreneurship in America's schools.* New York, NY: Dutton Books.

Meade, E. (1991). Foundations and the public schools. *Phi Delta Kappan 73* (2), K1-K12.

Ruskin, K., & Achilles, C. (1995). *Grantwriting, fundraising, and partnerships.* Thousand Oaks, CA: Corwin Press.

REFERENCES

Achilles, C., & Hoover, S. (1996). *Problem-based learning as a school-improvement vehicle.* Corpus Christi, TX: National Council of Professors of Educational Administration. (ERIC Document Reproduction Service No. ED 401 631).

Ackerman, R.H., Donaldson, G.A., & van der Bogert, R. (1996). *Making sense as a school leader: Persisting questions, creative opportunities.* San Francisco, CA: Jossey-Bass Publishers.

Ackland, R. (1991). A review of the peer coaching literature. *Journal of Staff Development, 12* (1), 22–27.

Adelman, N. E., Walking Eagle, K. P., & Hargreaves, A. (1997). Framing the cases: Time for change. In Adelman, N. E., Walking Eagle, K. P. & Hargreaves, A. (Eds.), *Racing with the clock: Making time for teaching and learning in school reform* (pp. 1–7). New York, NY: Teachers College Press.

Ashur, N. E., Babayco, M., Fullerton, J., Jackson, T., Jr., & Smith, K. (1991). An evaluation of the staff development program at College of the Canyons. (Report No. JC 920 247). East Lansing, MI: National Center for Research on Teacher Learning (ERIC Document Reproduction Service No. ED 345 771).

Baloche, L. A. (1998). *The cooperative classroom: Empowering learning.* Upper Saddle River, NJ: Prentice Hall.

Barott, J., & Raybould, R. (1998). Changing schools into collaborative organizations. In Pounder, D. G. (Ed.), *Restructuring schools for collaboration: Promises and pitfalls.* (pp. 27–42). Albany, NY: State University of New York Press.

Basom, R., & Crandall, D. (1991). Implementing a redesign strategy: Lessons from educational change. *Educational Horizons, 69* (2), 73–77.

Belasco, J. (1990). *Teaching the elephant to dance: Empowering change in your organization.* New York, NY: Crown Publishers.

Bell, C. R. (1986). How to establish effective staff development programs. *NASSP TIPS for Principals.* Reston, VA: National Association for Secondary School Principals.

Bennett, C. (1995). A staff development partnership for technology integration. *Journal of Staff Development, 16* (3), 19–22.

Bennis, W. (1989). *On becoming a leader.* Reading, MA: Addison-Wesley.

Blanchard, K., & Johnson, S. (1982). *The one minute manager: The quickest way to increase your own prosperity.* New York, NY: William Morrow and Company.

Blase, J., & Blase, J. (1998). *Handbook of instructional leadership: How really good principals promote teaching and learning.* Thousand Oaks, CA: Corwin Press.

Boggs, H. (1996). *Launching school change through teacher study groups: an Action research Paper.* Chicago, IL: Mid-Western Educational Research Association. (ERIC Document Reproduction Service No. ED 420 286).

Bradley, M. K., Kallick, B., & Regan, H. B. (1991). *The staff development manager: A guide to professional growth.* Boston, MA: Allyn & Bacon, Inc.

Brandt, R. (1982). On improving teacher effectiveness: A conversation with David Berliner. *Educational Leadership, 40* (1), 12–15.

Brennan, A. D. H., & Brennan, R. J. (1988). The principal, ethics, and special education. *National Association of Secondary School Principals Bulletin, 72* (512), 16–19.

Bridges, E. (1992). *Problem-based learning for administrators.* ERIC Clearinghouse on Educational management. Eugene, OR: University of Oregon.

Brookfield, S. D. (1986). *Understanding and facilitating adult learning.* San Francisco, CA: Jossey-Bass Publishers.

Brookfield, S.D. (1995). *Becoming a critically reflective teacher.* San Francisco, CA: Jossey-Bass Publishers.

Burden, P. (1982) *Developmental supervision: Reducing teacher stress at different career stages.* Paper presented at the Association of Teacher Educators National Conference, Phoenix, AZ.

Burke, P. J. , Christensen, J. C., & Fessler, R. (1984). *Teacher career stages: Implications for staff development.* Bloomington, IN: *Phi Delta Kappa Educational Foundation* Whole No. 214.

Caffarella, R. (1993). Facilitating self-directed learning as a staff development option. *Journal of Staff Development, 14* (2), 30–34.

Calabrese, R. L., & Zepeda, S. J. (1997). *The reflective supervisor: A practical guide for educators.* Larchmont, NY: Eye on Education.

Caldwell, S. (1989). Introduction. In S. Caldwell (Ed.), *Staff development: A handbook of effective practices* (pp. 9–13). Oxford, OH: National Staff Development Council.

Campbell, R., Corbally, J., & Ramseyer, J. (1958). *Introduction to educational administration.* Boston, MA: Allyn & Bacon.

Carnegie Forum on Education and the Economy. (1986). *A Nation prepared: The report of the task force on teaching as a profession.* New York, NY: Carnegie Forum. Author.

Carruthers, J. (1993). The principals and practice of mentoring. In B. J. Caldwell & E. M. A. Carter (Eds.), *The return of the mentor* (pp. 9–24). London: The Falmer Press.

Chell, J. (1995). Introducing principals to the role of instructional leadership. Unpublished master's thesis, Saskatchewan School Trustees Association, Regina, Saskatchewan, Canada.

Chesley, L. S., Wood, F., and Zepeda, S. J. (1997) Induction: Meeting the needs of the alternatively certified teacher. *Journal of Staff Development, 18* (1), 28–32.

Christen, W., & Murphy, T. (1987). Inservice training and peer evaluation: An integrated program for faculty development. *NASSP Bulletin, 71* (500), 10–18.

Christensen, J., Burke, P., Fessler, R., & Hagstrom, D. (1983). *Stages of teachers' careers: Implications for professional development.* Washington, DC: National Institute of Education (ERIC Document Reproduction Services No. ED 227 054).

Corey, S.(1953). *Action research to improve school practices.* New York, NY: Teachers College Press.

Costa, A., & Garmston, R. (1994). *Cognitive coaching: A foundation for renaissance schools.* Norwood, MA: Christopher-Gordon Publishers.

Costa, A., & Liebmann, R. (1997). Toward renaissance curriculum: An idea whose time has come. In A. Costa & R. Liebmann, (Eds.), *Envisioning process as content: Toward a renaissance curriculum* (pp. 1–20). Thousand Oaks, CA: Corwin Press.

Covey, S. R. (1989). *The seven habits of highly effective people.* New York: Simon & Schuster.

Covey, S. R. (1992). *Principle-centered leadership.* New York: Simon & Schuster.

Covey, S. R., Merrill, A., & Merrill, R. (1994), *First things first.* New York, NY: Simon & Schuster.

Cross, K.P. (1981). *Adults as learners: Increasing participation and facilitating learning.* San Francisco, CA: Jossey-Bass Publishers.

Crow, G. M., Matthews, L. J., & McCleary, L. E. (1996). *Leadership: A relevant and realistic role for principals.* Larchmont, NY: Eye on Education.

Dalellew, T. & Martinez, Y. (1988). Andragogy and development: A search for the meaning of staff development. *Journal of Staff Development, 9* (3), 28–31.

Danielson, C. (1996). *Enhancing professional practice: A framework for teaching.* Alexandria, VA: Association for Supervision and Curriculum Development.

Darling-Hammond, L., & Goodwin, A. L. (1993). Progress toward professionalism in teaching. (pp. 19–52). In G. Gordon Cawelti (Ed.), *Challenges and achievements of American education. 1993 Yearbook of the Association for Supervision and Curriculum Development* (pp. 19–52). Alexandria, VA: Association for Supervision and Curriculum Development.

Day, B. (1981). Foreword. In Dillion-Peterson, B. (Ed.), *Staff development/organization development*. Alexandria, VA: Association for Supervision and Curriculum Development.

de Luna, P. (1995). *The education foundation: Raising private funds for public schools* Eugene, OR: Oregon School Study Council. (ERIC Document Reproduction Service No. ED 390 152).

Dewey, J. (1933). *How we think*. Lexington, MA: D. C. Heath & Co.

Dewey, J. (1938). *Experience and education*. New York, NY: MacMillan.

Duke, D., & Corno, L. (1981). Evaluating staff development. In B. Dillion-Peterson (Ed.), *Staff development/organization development* (pp. 93–112). Alexandria, VA: Association for Supervision and Curriculum Development.

Edmonds, R. (1982). Programs of school improvement: An overview. *Educational Leadership, 40* (3), 4–11.

Ellis, T. I. (1986). The principal as instructional leader. NAESP, *Research Roundup, 3,* 1.

Engel, C. (1991). Not just a method, but a way of learning. In D. Boud & G. Feletti (Eds.), *The Challenge of Problem-based Learning* (pp. 23–33). New York, NY: St. Martin's Press.

Epperly, W., & Cohen, A. (1984). *Interactive career development: Integrating employer and employee goals*. New York, NY: Praeger.

Feiman, S., & Floden, R. (1980). *What's all this tale about teacher development*. East Lansing, MI: The Institute for Research on Teaching (ERIC Document Reproduction Service No. ED 189 088).

Forest, L. (1998). Cooperative learning communities: Expanding from classroom cocoon to global connections. In C. M. Brody & N. Davidson (Eds.), *Professional development for cooperative learning: Issues and approaches.* (pp. 287–306). Albany, NY: State University of New York Press.

Frazier, A. (1997). *A roadmap for quality transformation in education.* Boca Raton, FL: St. Lucie Press.

Fullan, M. (1982). *The meaning of educational change.* New York, NY: Teachers College Press.

Gage, N., & Berliner, D. (1988). *Educational psychology* (4th ed.). Dallas, TX: Houghton-Mifflin Co.

Gallagher, S. A., Stepien, W. J., & Rosenthal, H. (1992). The effects of problem-based learning on problem solving. *Gifted Child Quarterly, 36* (4), 195–200.

Ganser, T. (1996). What do mentors say about mentoring? *Journal of Staff Development, 17* (3), 36–39.

Gehrke, N. J. (1988). On preserving the essence of mentoring as one form of teacher leadership. *Educational Leadership, 39* (1), 43–45.

Gephart, M. A., Marsick, V. J., van Buren, M.E., & Spiro, M. S. (1996). Learning organizations come alive. *Training & Development, 50* (12), 35–45.

Gerstner, L., Semerad, R., Doyle, D., & Johnston, W. (1994). *Reinventing education: Entrepreneurship in America's schools.* New York, NY: Dutton Books.

Glanz, J. (1998). *Action research: An educational leader's guide to school improvement.* Norwood, MA: Christopher-Gordon Publishers.

Goodlad, J. (1979). *What schools are for.* Bloomington, IN: Phi Delta Kappan Educational Foundation.

Gredler, M. (1996). *Program evaluation.* Englewood Cliffs, NJ: Prentice-Hall.

Greene, M. (1988). *The dialectic of freedom*. New York, NY: Teachers College Press.

Griffin, G. A. (1983). Toward a conceptual framework for staff development. In G. A. Griffin (Ed.), *Staff development. Eighty-second Yearbook of the National Society for the Study of Education*. (pp. 228–250). Chicago, IL: The University of Chicago Press.

Guthrie, J., Garms, W., & Pierce L. (1988). *School finance and education policy: Enhancing educational efficiency, equality, and choice*. Englewood Cliffs, NJ: Prentice-Hall.

Hass, G. C. (1957). In-service education today. In N. B. Henry (Ed.), *In-service education: For teachers, supervisors, and administrators. The fifty-sixth yearbook of the National Society for the Study of Education*. (pp. 13–334). Chicago, IL: The University of Chicago Press.

Henry, T. (1995, June 7). Schools enriched by private funds. *The USA Today*. p. 4D.

Herzberg, F. (1968). One more time: How do you motivate employees? *Harvard Business Review, 46* (4), 53–62.

Hirsh, S., & Ponder, G. (1991). New plots, new heroes in staff development. *Educational Leadership, 49* (3), 43–48.

Hord, S., Rutherford, W., Huling-Austin, L., & Hall, G. (1987). *Taking charge of change*. Alexandria, VA: Association for Supervision and Curriculum.

Howey, K. R., & Vaughan, J. C. (1983). Current patterns of staff development. In G.A. Griffin (Ed.), *Staff development. Eighty-second yearbook of the National Society for the Study of Education*. (pp. 228–250). Chicago, IL: The University of Chicago Press.

Hoyle, J. R., & Crenshaw, H. M. (1997). *Interpersonal sensitivity*. Larchmont, NY: Eye on Education.

Jennings, D. F. (1993). *Effective supervision: Frontline management for the '90s*. Minneapolis, MN: West Publishing Company.

Joyce, B., & Calhoun, E. (1996). School renewal: An inquiry, not a prescription. In B. Joyce & E. Calhoun (Eds), *Learning experiences in school renewal: An exploration of five successful programs* (pp. 175–190). Eugene, OR: ERIC Clearinghouse on Educational Management.

Joyce, B., & Birdsall, L. (1977). *Inservice teacher education in California: Views of teachers.* Sacramento, CA: California State Department of Education. (ERIC Document Reproduction Service No. ED 160 570).

Joyce, B., & McKibbin, J. (1982). Teacher growth states and school environments *Educational Leadership, 40* (3), 32–36.

Joyce, B., & Showers, B. (1982). The coaching of teaching. *Educational Research, 40* (1), 4–8.

Joyce, B., & Showers, B. (1987). Low-cost arrangements for peer-coaching. *Journal of Staff Development, 8* (1), 22–24.

Keedy, J., & Thompson, E. (1988). *Evaluation of a staff development program.* Louisville, KY: Mid-South Educational Research Association (ERIC Document Reproduction Service No. ED 302 916).

Knowles, M.S. (1970). *The modern practice of adult education: Andragogy versus pedagogy.* New York, NY: Association Press.

Knox, A. B. (1977). *Adult development and learning: A handbook on individual growth and competence in the adult years.* San Francisco, CA: Jossey-Bass Publishers.

Kovic, S. (1996). Peer coaching to facilitate inclusion: A job-embedded staff development model. *Journal of Staff Development, 17* (1), 23–31.

Kraft, N. (1995) The dilemmas of deskilling: Reflections of a staff developer. *Journal of Staff Development, 16* (3), 31–34.

Laird, D. (1985). *Approaches to training and development.* Reading, MA: Addison-Wesley Publishing Company.

Lambert, L. (1995) Toward a Theory of Constructivist Leadership. In L. Lambert, D. Walker, D. Zimmerman, J. Cooper, M. Lambert, M. Gardner, & P. J. Ford-Slack (Eds.), *The constructivist leader* (pp. 28–51). New York, NY: Teachers College Press.

Langenbach, M. (1993). *Curriculum models of adult education.* Malabar, FL: Krieger Publishing Company.

Lee, G., & Barnett, B. (1994). Using reflective questioning to promote collaborative dialogue. *Journal of Staff Development, 15* (1), 16–21.

Lortie, D. (1965). Teacher socialization: The Robinson Crusoe Model. In *The real world of the beginning teacher* (pp. 35–74). Report of the Nineteenth National TEPS Conference. Washington, DC: National Education Association.

Makibbin, S., & Sprague, M. (1991). *Study Groups: Conduit for reform.* St. Louis, MO: National Staff Development Council. (ERIC Document Reproduction Service No. ED 370 893).

Marshak, D. (1997). *Action research on block scheduling.* Larchmont, NY: Eye on Education.

McBride, R., Reed, J., & Dollar, J. (1994). Teacher attitudes toward staff development: A symbolic relationship at best. *Journal of Staff Development, 15* (2), 36–41.

McCall, J. (1997). *The principal as steward.* Larchmont, NY: Eye on Education.

McKay, J. (1992). Professional development through action research. *Journal of Staff Development, 13* (1), 18–21.

Miner, J. (1997). *A psychological typology of successful entrepreneurs.* Westport, CT: Quorum Books.

Morgan, G. (1986). *Images of organizations.* Newbury Park, CA: Sage Publications, Inc.

Mortenson, R. & Grady, M. (1979). *Collaborative decision-making model for inservice education.* Paper presented to the American Association of Colleges for Teacher Education, Chicago, IL.

Munger, L. (1995). Job-embedded staff development in Norwalk schools. *Journal of Staff Development, 16* (3), 6–12.

Murphy, C. (1997). *Whole faculty study groups*. Paper presented at the National Staff Development Council Annual Conference. Nashville, TN.

Murphy, J., Murphy, C., Joyce, B., & Showers, B. (1988). The Richmond County school improvement program: Preparation and initial phase. *Journal of Staff Development, 9* (2), 36–41.

Murphy, J. (1990). The reform of school administration: Pressures and calls for change. In Murphy, J. (Ed.), *The educational reform movement of the 1980s* (pp. 277–303). Berkley, CA: McCutchan Publishing Co.

National Center for Education Statistics (1998). *Revenues and Expenditures for Public Elementary and Secondary Education: School Year 1995–1996* (NCES Publication No. 98–205). Washington, DC: U. S. Department of Education. Author.

National Council for Accreditation of Teacher Education (1995). *Standards procedures and policies for the accreditation of professional education units.* Washington, DC: Author.

National Staff Development Council. (1998). Standards for staff development. Oxford, OH: Author.

National Staff Development Council in Cooperation with the National Association of Elementary School Principals. (1998). Standards for staff development: Oxford, OH: National Staff Development Council. Author.

Neubert, G., & Bratton, E. (1987). Team coaching: Staff development side by side. *Educational Leadership, 44* (5), 29–32.

Newman, K., Burden, P., & Applegate, J. (1980). *Helping teachers examine their long-range development.* Washington, DC: Association of Teacher Educators (ERIC Document Reproduction Service No. ED 204 321).

Newman, K., Dornburg, B., Dubois, D., & Kranz, E. (1980). *Stress to teachers' midcareer transitions: A role for teacher education.* (ERIC Document Reproduction Services No. ED 196 868).

Newcomb, T. (1996). *Grants for beginners: The painless guide for teachers.* (Available from Dr. Thomas Newcomb, 19130 Nelson Parkman Road, Garrettsville, OH 44231).

Nicholson, A., Joyce, B., Parker, D., & Waterman, F. (1976). *The literature on inservice teacher education: An analytic review.* Washington, DC: National Center for Education Statistics. (ERIC Document Reproduction Service No. ED 129 734).

Norton, M., & Kelly, L. (1997). *Resource allocation: Managing money and people.* Larchmont, NY: Eye on Education.

Oja, S. & Smulyan, L. (1989). *Collaborative action research: a developmental approach.* London: The Falmer Press.

O'Neil, J. (1995). On schools as learning organizations: A conversation with Peter Senge. *Educational Leadership, 52* (7), 20–23.

O'Reilly, G., & Latimer, M. (1990). *Who teaches, who principals, who learns?* Victoria, BC, Canada: Canadian Society for Studies in Education. (ERIC Document Reproduction Service No. ED 324 770).

Orlich, D. (1989a). *Staff development.* Needham Heights, MA: Allyn & Bacon.

Orlich, D. (1989b). Evaluating staff development. *The Clearing House 62* (8), 370–374.

Pajak, E. (1993). *Approaches to clinical supervision: Alternatives for improving instruction.* Norwood, MA: Christopher-Gordon Publishers.

Palmer, P. J. (1998). *The courage to teach: Exploring the inner landscape of a teacher's life.* San Francisco, CA: Jossey-Bass Publishers.

Ponticell, J. A. (1995). Promoting teacher professionalism through collegiality. *Journal of Staff Development, 16* (3), 13–18.

Ponticell, J. A. (1997). Presentation: In-service: Project O.P.E.N. (Oklahoma Professional Educators Network), a joint Effort Between the University of Oklahoma and the Norman Public Schools.

Ponticell, J. A., & Zepeda, S. J. (1996). Making sense of teaching and learning: A case study of mentor and beginning teacher problem solving. In D. McIntyre & D. Byrd, (Eds.), *Preparing tomorrow's teachers: The field experience* (pp. 115–130). Thousand Oaks, CA: Corwin Press.

Razik, T. A., & Swanson, A. D. (1995). *Fundamental concepts of educational leadership and management.* Englewood Cliffs, NJ: Prentice Hall.

Reitzug, U. C., & Burrello, L. C. (1995). How principals can build self-renewing schools. *Educational Leadership, 52* (7), 48–50.

Report of the National Commission on Teaching and America's Future (1996). *What matters most: Teaching for America's future.* Washington, DC: U.S. Government Printing Office. Author.

Roberts, J. (1991). How to improve communication: A staff development mini-session. *Tips for Principals: National Association for Secondary School Principals.* Reston, VA: National Association of Secondary School Principals.

Ruskin, K. & Achilles, C. (1995). *Grantwriting, fundraising, and partnerships.* Thousand Oaks, CA: Corwin Press.

Rutherford, W. (1989). How to establish effective staff development programs. *Tips for Principals.* Reston, VA: National Association for Secondary School Principals.

Sage, S., & Torp, L. (1997). What does it take to become a teacher of problem-based learning? *Journal of Staff Development, 18* (4), 32–36.

Sanders, J. (1992). *Evaluating school programs.* Thousand Oaks, CA: Corwin Press.

Savery, J., & Duffy, T. (1995). Problem-based learning: An instructional model and its constructivist framework. *Educational Technology, 35* (5), 31–38.

Schlechty, P. (1997). *Inventing better schools.* San Francisco, CA: Jossey-Bass Publishers.

Schön, D. (1987). *Educating the reflective practitioner.* San Francisco, CA: Jossey-Bass Publishers.

Seifert, E., & Simmons, D. (1997). Learning centered schools using a problem-based approach. *NASSP Bulletin, 81* (587), 90–97.

Senge, P. M. (1990). *The fifth discipline: The art and practice of the learning organization.* New York, NY: Currency Doubleday.

Senge, P. M. (1996). Leading learning organizations. In F. Hesselbein, M. Goldsmith, & R. Beckhard (Eds.), *The leader of the future: New visions, strategies, and practices for the next era* (pp. 41–58). San Francisco, CA: Jossey-Bass Publishers.

Senge, P. M., Kleiner, A., Roberts, C., Ross, R.B., & Smith, B.J. (1994). *The fifth discipline field book: Strategies and tools for building a learning organization.* New York: Doubleday.

Sergiovanni, T. J. (1992). *Moral leadership: Getting to the heart of school improvement.* San Francisco, CA: Jossey-Bass Publishers.

Sergiovanni, T.J. (1994). Cultural and competing perspectives in administrative theory and practice. In T.J. Sergiovanni & J.E. Corbally (Eds.), *Leadership and organizational culture* (pp. 1–12). Chicago: University of Illinois Press.

Sergiovanni, T. J. (1996). *Leadership for the schoolhouse: How is it different? Why is it important?* San Francisco, CA: Jossey-Bass Publishers.

Setteducati, D. (1995). Portfolio self-assessment for teachers: A reflection on Farmingdale. *Journal of Staff Development, 16* (3), 2–5.

Showers, B. (1985). Teachers coaching teachers. *Educational Leadership, 42* (7), 43–48.

Smith, E., & Tyler, R. (1942). *Appraising and recording student progress.* New York, NY: Harper and Brothers.

Sparks, D., & Hirsh, S. (1997). *A new vision for staff development.* Alexandria, VA: Association for Supervision and

Curriculum Development and Oxford, OH: National Staff Development Council.

Sparks, D., & Loucks-Horsley, S. (1989). Five models of staff development for teachers. *Journal of Staff Development, 10* (4), 40–57.

Starratt, R. J. (1996). *Transforming educational administration: Meaning, community, and excellence.* New York, NY: McGraw-Hill.

Storeygard, J., & Fox, B. (1995). Reflections on video: One teacher's story. *Journal of Staff Development, 16* (3), 25–29.

Sweeney, J. (1982). Research synthesis on effective school leadership. *Educational Leadership, 39* (5), 346–352.

Thompson, D., & Wood, C. (1998). *Money and schools: A handbook for practitioners.* Larchmont, NY: Eye on Education.

Thurston, P., Clift, R., & Schacht, M. (1993). Preparing leaders for change-oriented schools. *Phi Delta Kappan, 75* (3), 259–265.

Torp, L. & Sage, S. (1998). *Problems as possibilities: Problem-based learning for K-12 education.* Alexandria, VA: Association for Supervision and Curriculum Development.

Tracy, S., & Schuttenberg, E. (1990). Promoting teacher growth and school improvement through self-directed learning. *Journal of Staff Development, 11* (2), 52–57.

Van Meter, E., & Murphy, J. (1997, July). *Using ISLLC standards to strengthen preparation programs in school administration.* Paper presented for the Interstate Leaders Licensure Consortium. Washington DC: Council of Chief State School Officers. Author.

Van Ness, C., & Van Ness, J. (1978). *Winning foundation and corporate grants* Washington, DC: National Council for Resource Development. (ERIC Document Reproduction Service No. ED 162 695).

Watson, D., & Stevenson, M.. (1989). Teacher support groups: Why and how. In G. Pinnell & M. Matlin (Eds.), *Teachers and research: Language learning in the classroom* (pp. 121–122). Newark, DE: International Reading Association.

Wolf, R. (1990). *Evaluation in education: Foundations of competency assessment and program review.* (3rd Ed.). New York, NY: Praeger Publishers.

Wollman-Bonilla, J. (1997). Mentoring as a two-way street. *Journal of Staff Development, 18* (3), 50–52.

Wood, F. H. (1989). Organizing and managing school-based staff development. In S. D. Caldwell (Ed.). *Staff development: A handbook of effective practices* (pp. 26–43). Oxford, OH: National Staff Development Council.

Wood, F. H., Killian, J., McQuarrie, F. O., & Thompson, S. (1993). *How to organize a school-based staff development program.* Alexandria, VA: Association for Supervision and Curriculum Development.

Wood, F. H., & Thompson, S. (1993). Assumptions about staff development: Based on research and best practice. *Journal of Staff Development, 14* (1), 52–57.

Wood, F. H., & Killian, J. (1998). Job-embedded learning makes the difference in school improvement. *Journal of Staff Development, 19* (1), 52–54.

Wood, F. H., Thompson, S., & Russell, F. (1981). Designing effective staff development programs. In Dillion-Peterson, B. (Ed.), *Staff Development/Organization Development.* Alexandria. VA: Association for Supervision and Curriculum Development.

Zemke, R., & Zemke, S. (1995). Adult learning: What do we know for sure? *Training, 32* (6), 31–40.

Zepeda, S., Wood, F., & O'Hair, M. (1996). A vision of supervision for 21st century schooling. *Wingspan, 11* (2), 26–30.

Zey, M. (1984) *The mentor connection.* Homewood, IL: Dow-Jones-Irving.